*To*

IDA  THALLON  HILL

SCHOLAR — FRIEND

# Our Debt to Greece and Rome

EDITORS
GEORGE DEPUE HADZSITS, PH.D.

DAVID MOORE ROBINSON, PH.D., LL.D.

Narra Apuleo, che (mentr' eoli cangiato
In Afino feruiua à genti ladre)
Vna fpofa rubbaro, il deftinato
Didele nozze le rapaci fquadre,

Cui (per farle fcordare un fogno ingrato)
Dona conforto una canuta madre,
Che l'hauea in guardia & con grata fauella
Le racconta di Pfiche la nouella.

THE TELLING OF THE STORY OF CUPID AND PSYCHE
Engraved by Agostino Veneziano from the design of Michiel van Coxie

# APULEIUS
# AND HIS INFLUENCE

BY

ELIZABETH HAZELTON HAIGHT, Ph.D.

COOPER SQUARE PUBLISHERS, INC.

NEW YORK

1963

Published 1963 by Cooper Square Publishers, Inc.
59 Fourth Avenue, New York 3, N. Y.
Library of Congress Catalog Card No. 63-10290

PRINTED IN THE UNITED STATES OF AMERICA

# PRESENTING APULEIUS

PERMIT me to introduce to you, Ladies and Gentlemen, my distinguished friend, Apuleius of Madaura. I am aware that a few of you have met him before; I surmise that to many he is unknown; I am convinced that he will challenge the interest of all.

You ask: " Who is this person? " as his hero Lucius says. Hear in a few words: A gentleman born in Africa, educated in Carthage, Athens and Rome, who lived in the second century of our era, and had a varied career as lawyer, sophist and litterateur.

Why do I introduce him? Because to me his works are modern, stimulating and of infinite variety from his interests in men, women and romance; in science, magic, religion and philosophy. Why do I think you should know him? Because from Bottom back to Lucius every man with an ass's head may owe something to Apuleius; because some of the best and raciest stories of the few plots in the world dropped from his pen; because in the literature and art of Europe in almost every country you are

[ vii ]

bound to meet adaptations and illustrations of his lovely story of Cupid and Psyche.

I will admit frankly that he is difficult to understand, elusive, subtle, enveloped in mysteries. I cannot guarantee his moral character, or certify his good taste, or clear him from the charge of having practiced magic. I can affirm, however, in his own words, that studied he will give you joy.

*Lector, intende; laetaberis.*

# CONTENTS

[ ix ]

# CONTENTS

# ILLUSTRATIONS

[ xi ]

# APULEIUS
## AND HIS INFLUENCE

# APULEIUS
# AND HIS INFLUENCE

## I. THE AGE OF THE ANTONINES

THE approximate dates of Apuleius, 125–171 A.D., place him in the time of Antoninus Pius and Marcus Aurelius. Born in Africa, educated in Carthage, Athens and Rome, a traveller to the east, lawyer, sophist, novelist, scientist and philosopher, Apuleius is essentially the child of that modern Graeco-Roman world which he represented in his bilingual literary work. Versatile, restless, curious, unsatisfied, seeking now expression for his own subtle inner life, now some solution for the mysteries of the outer world, he is as Protean as he is fascinating and in his own personal metamorphoses suggests something of the spiritual transformations which the Roman Empire was undergoing during this epoch.

The changes in the Roman world were not apparent in the time of Antoninus Pius, for the reign was uneventful. The Emperor by his charitableness, loyalty and nobility won from the Senate the epithet of *Pius* which forever associated him with Aeneas in devotion to the state and reverence for the gods. Frugal in his personal habits, beneficent to the poor, informal with his subjects, he centered his life in Italy working to perfect Roman jurisprudence for the benefit of the state, then loving to retire to the simple life of his country estate in Etruria, and not perhaps having that more cosmopolitan viewpoint which had made his predecessor, Hadrian, travel constantly in the provinces. Turning instinctively to the great past of Rome, he sought to maintain the *mos maiorum,* her traditional morality, to encourage an archaistic literature which should revive the purity of republican speech; and to establish the laws by clearer codification. It was typical of the sovereign and his time that when death approached, although the menace of border wars was rising like a black cloud, he gave the watchword " Equanimity " before breathing his last. The character sketch of him written by his adopted son, Marcus Aurelius, pictures a self-controlled, public-spirited, genial gentleman, a wise, unselfish and enlightened ruler.

[ 4 ]

No such calm marked the reign of Marcus Aurelius, although the Emperor seemed Plato's very Philosopher-King, destined to inaugurate the millenium of the world. There is no more tragic figure in the line of Roman sovereigns. Two self-revelations which he left portray by contrast the struggle of a brooding soul caught in the meshes of unavoidable public activities. In the correspondence with Fronto, the great rhetorician and archaistic writer who was his tutor, we see a temperamental youth, extravagant in devotion to his master, over-zealous in studies, later exuberant in love for his wife and for his dear nestlings, their children, in revolt against the technicalities and dryness of formal rhetoric, and even forsaking his dear master's art of words for the pure study of philosophy, the art of living. In these Latin letters, brief as they are, there is the zest for life, or life itself. The *Meditations*, written in Greek during the war with the Quadi, are the searching self-analysis and criticism of a weary and lonely soul, fighting against War, Pestilence and Disillusion for its Stoic faith in divine wisdom and human goodness. In camp in the far north, the Emperor makes solemn review of the influences in his life, of his spiritual debts to parents, wife and teachers, and then over and over he reiterates his faith in that dominant Reason manifest in all the changing flux of the world, and in the power of man to be so at one with the flow that his life, like God's, shall be harmonious, victorious over evil and pain, far-seeing, calm. For thus by repetition and mental control Marcus Aurelius sought to retire from the military and civic disasters of his reign to his inner citadel, where he could find rest and strength to go on again with his great task.

For the Philosopher could theoretically make evil naught but the Ruler could not end public or private distress. Throughout his reign there were frontier wars against the Parthians, against the German tribes, against the Sarmatians. And at home there was an even more destructive enemy in the plague brought back from Parthia by the soldiers. Also, in the midst of the miseries of his people Marcus Aurelius had little personal support, for his nearest props tottered. His wife's virtue was said to be not above reproach. Lucius Verus, his adoptive brother, whom with more generosity than statesmanship he had made " co-Caesar " with himself, succumbed to the lure of the East at Antioch. One of his most successful generals,

[ 6 ]

Avidius Cassius, revolted against him. His son and heir, Commodus, was to prove thoroughly unworthy. The reputation of his daughter, Lucilla, was like that of her mother. But it is not mere personal tragedy that the Emperor is fighting through in his *Meditations:* it is rather the world struggle, re-current generation after generation, which he seeks to lighten through the thought of immanent Reason and man's oneness with God.

But the life of the Emperor is far from being a complete picture of the time, and the resigned fortitude of the Stoic was not an adequate solution or balm for all the convulsed world. The people, freedmen and slaves, were forging onward to a life of their own and in Petronius' *Satyricon* had already found a place in literature. They were working out their social life through the guilds and the coöperative burial societies, however much these were restricted by law and suspected by emperors. On the other hand, the nobles, who had amassed great fortunes in the years of prolonged peace, felt increasing philanthropic responsibility to devote a portion of their wealth to the public good, and as it was a time when the populace, masses and nobles alike, demanded entertainment, such benefactions often took the form of buildings destined for shows or of the production of gladiatorial combats. And this was true not only of Rome, but of many other cities in Italy and in the provinces, since the growth of municipal life fostered the production of multitudinous small copies of " the City," as Rome was called. To Marcus Aurelius the gladiatorial combats might be distasteful and the drama so tedious that he read his books at the theater when his presence seemed essential, but the people in every city wished such amusements, and the poor expected both *panem et circenses* so that "the bread-line" was continually an ancient problem as it is a modern.

The East was pouring into Italy, now that Rome was the mistress of the Mediterranean, and with the influx of many men of foreign blood, new ideas, new emotions, new aspirations were scattered like seed throughout the peninsula and grew apace in its fertile soil, for the time was ripe for change. In no field is this so clear as in the field of religion. Rather, I should say, in the growing interest in superstitions, religious cults and various philosophies.

In his essay *On Superstition* Plutarch had urged men to combat this " state of opinion

charged with emotion and productive of fear "
as something far worse than atheism. Plutarch
did not there discuss the particular forms of
superstition rife in his time, but a host of
phantoms can be invoked instantly as the background to his reflections and familiar also in
the age of the Antonines: Astrology with men's
horoscopes in her hands, Divination with her
clairvoyant powers, Dreams with their subtle
interpretations, Oracles old and new, Epiph-
anies of the Gods, Miracles, Sorcery. Such were
the multiplex lures to credulity which the simple-
minded accepted and with which the intellectuals experimented. Read the Sacred Orations
of the fanatic Aristides, the treatise of Artemi-
dorus on the interpretation of dreams, and the
life of the impostor Alexander of Abonoteichus,
who established a new oracle. After such histories it is not strange to find on the column of
Marcus Aurelius in Rome in the chiseled spiral
record of his wars a picture of the Miracle of
the Rain by which in one battle his foes were
confounded: the work of an Egyptian sorcerer,
says the historian Cassius Dio — nay, of the
soldiers in the Christian legion, the " Thunder-
ing," corrects the monk Xiphilinus, for they
brought down rain by prayer to their God.

Apuleius himself is closely associated with the magic of the time and nowhere more clearly than in his *Metamorphoses* is depicted or suggested the intimate connection of magic with religion and the vague line of demarcation drawn between their concepts. In the *Metamorphoses* Lucius' quest for knowledge of the unknown runs the gamut of change from magic incantations, through foul orgies of Syrian priests, to ecstatic worship of Egyptian gods. Apuleius' hero is typical of the age. The cold formality of the pristine Roman religion had lost its hold long ago. The bright Greek deities with their beautiful myths were old stories now and sceptics like Lucian were conveying in popular writings the absurdities of gods created in the image of men. Yet even the greatest scientists of the time, Ptolemy of Alexandria and Galen of Pergamum, acknowledged the power and the usefulness of astrology. And only a few of the intellectuals could live without some form of faith. The age was ripe for new cults that would satisfy individual craving for emotional relief. Therefore more and more influence was being achieved by the gods of the Orient, who had indeed appeared in Italy earlier, had been rejected, had returned, had bided their time: Isis of the Myriad Names with Osiris of the Water of Healing; the Great Mother of Phrygia with her self-dedicated Atthis; Mithras the ever-victorious young warrior. And these new cults by consecrated priests, regular services, mystic ceremonies, ecstatic initiations and promises of immortality warmed, enlivened and comforted world-worn hearts. Christianity too was steadily gaining ground with the intelligentsia and the powerful as well as with the uneducated poor; indeed in two centuries more, in spite of the persecutions of Christians at this time, it was to be recognized as the official religion of the Roman empire.[1]

All these new religions were colorful rivals to the philosophical systems which too were making their appeal to the jaded intellects of men through preaching, lecturing, writing. The Cynic Peregrinus, the Peripatetic Claudius Severus, the Platonist Sextus of Chaeronea, with their various theories of man's way of life and adjustment to the outer world, were offering to their hearers the mendicant friar's wallet and staff, the scientist's investigations, or the idealist's vision of the unseen realities back of all visible forms. And these philosophical theories no less than religious faith had their martyrs, so that a Peregrinus lay down on his self-kindled pyre to prove absolutely his contempt of death; while in the reigns of Nero and Domitian the great Stoics faced execution with a calm *non dolet*.

Thus in the age of the Antonines there appears the startling phenomenon of a populace wild over gladiatorial exhibitions and gloating over the sight of death in games, and yet so impressed by the supernatural and the interlacing of an invisible world with this tangible one that many, according to their mentality and temperament, were trying to interpret life's mysteries through magic, astrology, divination, religion and philosophy. It was this yearning in all classes of people toward the unknown that gave necromancer, soothsayer and philosophic missionary the opportunity for receptive hearings. It was the desire to be entertained, not always instructed, that furnished enthusiastic audiences for the displays of the sophists. Never was the rivalry between philosopher and rhetorician for the world's ear more keen. The restless time must have activity: shows, travel, acrobatic word performances, voyages into the unknown.

The life in the provinces was in many ways like that in Italy. What Greece was in this period is partly portrayed in the lives of three men who were working along very different lines: Pausanias, Herodes Atticus, Lucian. Pausanias, a Greek of Asia Minor who had travelled widely, conceived the idea of writing a description of all Greece, apparently to serve as a guide-book for those who wished to know the country. Perhaps patriotic motives made him perceive that such knowledge of Greece would help in that Grecizing of the Roman Empire which had evoked Horace's epigram: "Captive Greece took captive her fierce conqueror." Though he wrote for the Romans and described the great structures erected by Hadrian in Athens and the building activity of Herodes Atticus in his own time, his interests in Greece were mainly, as Frazer points out, antiquarian and religious, so that he dwells upon historic monuments of the glorious free days of Greece and lingers over the art of the fifth and fourth centuries before Christ. Frazer in his remarkable introduction to his distinguished edition of Pausanias shows that he represents the point of view of the average Intellectual of his time: as a man who believed in

the gods and their oracles even when he tried
to rationalize many myths about them; as a
man of common sense who, "while he looked
back with regret to the great age of Greek freedom, appears to have acquiesced in the Roman
dominion as inevitable, acknowledging the in-
capacity of the degenerate Greeks to govern
themselves, the general clemency of the Roman
rule, and especially the wisdom and beneficence
of the good emperors under whom it was his
happiness to live; " yet he was not " a stranger
to those graver thoughts on the vaster issues of
life and history which the aspect of Greece in
its decline was fitted to awake." Witness his
simple roll-call of the great Greek dead in the
Ceramicus, the national burying-ground of
Athens, and the poignant tribute that he pays.
It is no less the simplicity, clarity and dignity of
Pausanias' narrative than the scope of his enter-
prise which makes his description of Greece,
still the guide-book of the thoughtful traveller,
one of the greatest national monuments of
Greece in the second century.

Herodes Atticus of Marathon illustrates the
phenomenal careers of sophists at this time. A
*fortunae filius* with a wealthy father and wife,
he chose to follow the rhetorician's calling and

taught first at Athens, then at Rome. Marcus
Aurelius was among his pupils and his fame was
so great that he was made consul by Antoninus
Pius in 143 A.D. After that honor, however, he
chose instead of preferment at Rome life at
Athens, and continued his public career in
Greece, having at one time the administration
of the free towns of Asia. His brilliant successes
aroused envy: perhaps his own arrogance, as
his biographer Philostratus says, instigated an
appeal to Marcus Aurelius against him; in any
case he had to defend his reputation before the
Emperor at Sirmium and, though exonerated,
afterwards left public life and retired to his Villa
Cephisia near Marathon. He is memorialized
not by his rhetorical writings which have perished, but by the record of his philanthropic
building activity throughout Greece, in Asia
Minor and in Italy, and by the ruins of some of
his magnificent edifices. The stadium in Athens
which he embellished with marble, though rebuilt, recalls him. The magnificent ruins of his
Odeum below the southwest angle of the Acropolis attest the honor which he paid to his wife's
memory in the erection of this colossal theater,
or music hall. His name, though its brilliancy is
tarnished by Philostratus' gossiping anecdotes,

[ 15 ]

recalls the rhetorician's eloquence and the philanthropist's beneficences.

Lucian of Samosata had a career in letters of far greater and more varied brilliancy than that of Herodes, and like him received political honors, though these came so late in life that they fortunately did not interfere with his literary work. The Greek of his voluminous writing is so thoroughly clear, simple and "classical" that it would hardly seem believable that it was a language acquired by a Syrian if we had not seen the phenomenon of Joseph Conrad's English in our own time. His extant works represent all phases of his literary life: first, as rhetorician, then as philosopher, then as a "literary Prometheus" (in his own words), fusing Comedy and Dialogue into a dramatic satire which gave him his unique and suitable form for the criticism of contemporary life. For in these dialogues, whether he was influenced as he was at different periods by the writers of the New Attic Comedy, by the Menippean satires or by the Old Comedy, he was holding a mirror up to his age and then questioning the significance of all the phases of the life of the times. No keener goad to the duty of thinking had been plied in Greece since Socrates himself taught the searching method of the Questioner. Rhetoric itself, religion, philosophy and ethics, in one form of literature or another, become the subjects of Lucian's interest. So he shows the superficialities and vanities of the rhetorician's art; he turns his ironic comment on superstition and on sacrifices; he lets the gods talk in little, vain, passionate dialogues to show that they are but human creations made in man's own image; he writes of one philosophical creed after another, with apparent desire to penetrate into the very soul of each and expose its most intimate fastness; and then, " sworn to follow the dictates of no one master," he is off to diatribes against such spiritual servitude as comes from accepting salaried posts in great Roman houses.

His irony, his destructive criticism, his hard brilliancy, his rhetorical flare would, untempered, make him a rather unattractive figure, but his passion for sincerity of thought and independence of spirit, his love for quiet Athens, finally his humor and self-irony give him a magnetic appeal. It is a lofty spirit that wrote the delicate satire of " The Dependent Scholar " — the Greek rhetorician as parasite at Romans' tables; it is a true Greek who, though born a Syrian, could contrast so tellingly in his "Nigrinus" life in Rome where pleasure enters by the gate of every sense, where wealth and megalomania dominate and the world is a hodge-podge of informers, flatterers, diners, murderers, legacy-hunters, false friends, light women, — and life in Athens where Philosophy and Poverty are fellow-citizens with men, where freedom of spirit, quiet and leisure are more valued than gold.

Pausanias and Lucian are the names which make Greece still seem great in the Antonine age, but in their own writings appears much of the sad deterioration of the country: the depopulation, the miseries of the poor, the need for truckling to the Roman conquerors, the resultant depression. In the province of Africa, there was more resiliency, more of a forward look. Greece, gazing back to the golden days of Pericles, in painful toils produced a satirist. Africa, increasingly prosperous and magnificent, was finding new expression in the language of her lords, and producing that *elocutio novella* which was to have such influence on the linguistic children of Rome. And Africa, demanding in the fullness of life that above all she be entertained, gave birth to Apuleius, the writer of a great romance.

It is almost necessary to go to Africa today
to see from the extensive ruins uncovered by the
French and the Italians how Rome rebuilt and
restored what she had destroyed in the Punic
Wars. The history of the country from the raz-
ing of Carthage in 146 B.C. to the time of Marcus Aurelius reveals first Rome fighting with
Numidia and conquering it, attempting to leave
autonomy to Mauritania, then finding it necessary to take possession also of that district and
then of another, until under Caligula all Africa
was Roman. Then to maintain the *pax romana*
in the province one legion, the third Augustan,
was quartered there under Vespasian, and, established first at Thereste, then at Lambaesis,
it attained from its permanency such a life of
its own that Lambaesis became a *municipium*
under Marcus Aurelius, the *res publica Lam-
baesitanorum,* whose history may be studied
from ruins and inscriptions. But before Marcus Aurelius, the good emperors had been
deeply interested in Africa, Trajan had founded
Timgad, whose ruins today show the typical
Africo-Roman city with forum, basilica, theater, capitolium, baths, triple arch to emperor.
Hadrian visited the camp at Lambaesis and left
as a monument in Africa more magnificent

than his arch at Oea or the gateway at Sufetula, the great aqueduct which brought water from Mounts Zaghonan and Djongar to Carthage and Tunis. Carthage, rebuilt on the site of the old city in the time of Augustus, the seat of the proconsul of Africa, had attained in this second century A.D. its greatest splendor.

For in this time the *pax romana* seemed fairly secure. Native tribes of Libyans were allowed to continue their tribal organization with a headman responsible to the Empire. Punic towns changed their *suffetes* or two chief officials, for the government of *duoviri* and *decuriones* without serious difficulty. Many colonists established new communities. Commerce was developed by new trade routes and the use of camels for transportation. Corn and oil were among the chief exports and from the time of Augustus the quarrying of marble was an important industry. The land was controlled in general by imperial holdings or large estates, *saltus,* and that the condition of the serfs was pitiful is seen from various kinds of evidence. In Trajan's time the Africans appealed directly to the Emperor against the Proconsul and his subordinate officer; the case, which was heard by the Emperor himself, lasted during a three-days' session of the Senate, and Pliny and Tacitus, who appeared as lawyers for the provincials, were successful in their prosecution. The punishment of these corrupt officials could not end all such oppression, and again in the time of Commodus a pitiful appeal came from the colonists to the Emperor: " We are only poor peasants. We earn our living by the sweat of our brows. Have pity on us poor sons of the soil, and let us not be molested by the tax-gatherers on the estate." [2]

Life in the municipalities presents a more brilliant aspect, for here the prosperity of the well-to-do exhibited itself in the embellishment of the town and in a gaiety which copied the elegant brilliancy of Rome. And the annals of the poor are less evident. Timgad may be studied as a typical small city. But Carthage, as the city of Africa, the sister of Rome, *soror civitas,* and the one most intimately associated with Apuleius' career, may represent for us the height of African splendor.

The excavations which have long been carried on by the French [2a] are bringing to light traces of Punic, Roman and Christian Carthage and help to revivify the history of the city, but the actual ruins give no such idea of the splendor of the Roman city as do the literary sources. The site today as of old shows the magnificent Byrsa or Acropolis towering up between sea and lake, the far view of the Mediterranean, the inland hills and fertile plains. On this high Byrsa were some of the great public buildings, Praetorium (official residence of the Proconsul), Curia, Basilicae, besides various temples. Notable were the Temple of Aesculapius with its public library, and the Temple of Caelestis, the goddess of Carthage. Two harbors provided for merchant and war vessels. Forum, circus, amphitheater, stadium, palaestra, baths were numbered among the city's buildings. These public edifices and the houses of the rich were elegantly decorated with the African marbles, while the houses of the poor were of tufa. The streets were narrow, the buildings high, some of the houses rising six or seven stories.

The very list of buildings suggests how Romanized the city was, how prosperous, how pleasure-loving. And literature and the pictorial art of the mosaics, so popular in Africa, show the splendor of banquets, the delight in gladiatorial combats, in horse-racing, in theatrical performances and music. Apuleius in fragments

of his speeches pictures for us the theater with
its marble floors, high stage with columns back
of it, extensive tiers of seats and the various
performances which went on there: mimes,
comedies, tragedies, exhibitions of jugglers,
rope-walkers, and dancers, finally the displays
of the rhetorician's art. He begs his audience
to transfer their minds from theater to senate-
house if he speaks words worthy of it; or to
public library if his utterances are learned
enough.

Again he speaks of using the Persian baths
for a sprained ankle; of the Temple of Aesculapius, where the god honors the citadel of
Carthage with his very presence; of honorary
statues erected to illustrious citizens; of the
distinction of the senators of Carthage; of
the learning of her citizens. We shall see how
the *Florida,* the fragments of his rhetorical
speeches, reflect the brilliant life of this greatest
city in Africa, and as we read Apuleius we shall
find him peculiarly the child of the Antonine
age, the joint product of Carthage, Athens and
Rome.

## II. THE LIFE OF APULEIUS

THE life of Apuleius confounds any biographer's attempts at serious treatment, because in itself it resembles nothing so much as a mystery story or a melodrama, and because Apuleius' own humor made him choose to appear as a fantastic, clad in the garb of various subtle rôles. No other Latin author is so much of the twentieth century in love of excitement and sensation, passion for travel, pragmatic acceptance of every method of obtaining knowledge, interest in the psychic, and finally self-expression as magnetic and popular lecturer. His works present the anomaly of self-portraiture sketched with few outlines of fact, but much color of personality, so that the man becomes real to us while the questions about his life remain unanswered. Through his extant writings he is revealed as romantic novelist, brilliant lawyer, popular lecturer and Platonic philosopher, and through his many styles he presents an unparalleled picture of life in the second century of our era.

If his biographer could convey Apuleius' own personality with all its color, its verve, its multiplex interests and its manifold expressions, the biographer too would have a right to repeat Apuleius' own invitation: " Reader, give attention: you will be entertained."

Frank confession of many gaps in knowledge about his life is at once necessary. It is not possible to be certain about his first name or what language he spoke as a child; when he was born or when he died; whether he had a son; when he wrote his greatest work, the romance called *Metamorphoses;* whether he is the hero of it, and whether it is pure fiction or allegory; whether he was acquitted in his trial for practicing magic arts, and whether he really was a magician as Saint Augustine and the Middle Ages believed.

The main sources of knowledge about Apuleius' life are his own writings: the *Metamorphoses,* a story of the adventures of a man Lucius, who was turned into an ass; the *Apologia,* his speech for his own defense when he was accused of having won a rich wife by magic arts; the *Florida,* short extracts made from his public speeches on many lecture platforms, and his philosophical writings, largely based on

Plato. It is probable or at least possible that this was the order in which these books were written, as Rohde's exhaustive study has tried to show, and the assumption gives a reasonable working hypothesis for tracing the development of Apuleius' personality and thought.

The birthplace of Apuleius was Madaura, a flourishing Roman colony in the province of Africa, about eighty miles east of Cirta, the old Numidian capital, and on the border between Numidia and Gaetulia, so that Apuleius humorously describes himself as semi-Numidian, semi-Gaetulian. His father was the leading citizen of the town, and had held office as one of the two duumvirs, the chief officials in the *colonia*. Owing to his father's position, Apuleius was able to attend meetings of the senate, as sons of decurions could without participating in its business, but according to Saint Augustine Apuleius himself never attained any political office.

What language Apuleius first spoke is uncertain. It may have been Punic since his stepson Pudens spoke that. It was more probably Latin but a provincial dialect, since he had to work hard on the Latin language when he went to Rome in young manhood. He may also have known Greek early, for Greek was in common use in Africa, and the letter of Apuleius' wife which was produced in his trial was written in Greek. At some time he and his brother inherited from their father a fortune of 2,000,000 sesterces, and this must have been in early life as Apuleius says he diminished his patrimony by his prolonged education and extensive travels, as well as by generous gifts to friends and teachers.

His elementary education must have been received at Madaura, but after that he studied at Carthage, Athens and Rome. Carthage at this time was the city re-founded by Augustus, peaceful, wealthy, luxurious, with many great public buildings. In several speeches, Apuleius refers to Carthage with great devotion, and proudly claims to be her foster-son, since here his childhood was spent, his education was begun, and his philosophical thought, afterwards developed at Athens, was started. In a burst of rhetoric he declares that all citizens of Carthage are learned, Carthage is the celestial Greek Muse of Africa, the Roman Muse of all wearers of the toga.

The scope of his education is picturesquely described by the African in this same speech.

" There is a famous saying of a wise man about the delights of dining: 'the first wine bowl quenches thirst, the second produces merriment, the third leads to pleasure, the fourth to madness.' But the bowls of the Muses have a different effect. For the more you quaff and the stronger the better is it for your soul's health. So the first bowl, proffered by the elementary teacher, stimulates the beginning of study, the second of the teacher of literature instructs by training, the third of the rhetorician arms by eloquence. These potations content the majority. But I have drunk other cups at Athens: the elegant draught of poetry, the clear cup of geometry, the sweet one of music, the stiff one of dialectic, and the inexhaustible nectar of universal philosophy."

Thus Apuleius had gone through the complete cycle of education in the schools of *litterator, grammaticus, rhetor, philosophus,* and was ready to pursue knowledge in all fields and to write in any literary form. He had received the disciplinary training in which he believed, and in his ardor for learning he had devoted himself to his studies from youth up, he says, scorning all pleasures, even injuring his good health in extravagant labor by day and by night. Now

because of his hard toil he could stand up in the
court-room at Sabrata and claim before Claudius Maximus that he had a right to some
reputation in the fields of oratory and philosophy.

Before, however, he delivered his famous
*Apologia*, he had studied several years in
Athens, had travelled in the East, for he speaks
of having seen Samos and Hierapolis in Phrygia
at some time, had been initiated at Cenchreae,
near Corinth, in the mysteries of Isis, had gone
to Rome and there (if we may regard Book XI
of the *Metamorphoses* as partly autobiographical) had twice again been initiated in the mysteries of the Egyptian goddess and Osiris, had
pleaded cases to secure funds for the expenses
of these religious rites and had probably written
his great novel.

Then the *Wanderlust* started him off again
and he came to Oea on his way to Alexandria.
There he fell into the fateful illness which
brought upon him matrimony and a host of
troubles. Oea was on the coast of Africa near
the modern Tripoli, and it became significant in
Apuleius' life because it was the home of Sicinius Pontianus, an old school-friend of his at
Athens.

So far the life of Apuleius had been quiet in tenor though varied in scene. But here at Oea the melodrama began. Pontianus was looking for a second husband for his mother, Pudentilla, a rather strange proceeding, but explicable. Pudentilla had been left a widow by her husband, Sicinius Amicus, fourteen years before, with two small sons to bring up. She had devoted her youth and energy to their interests and the protection of their property, even going so far as to succumb to pressure from her first husband's relatives to become engaged to her brother-in-law, Sicinius Clarus, a feeble old man, when her father-in-law threatened not to leave his property to her sons if she did not yield to his wishes. Providentially the father-in-law died before so distasteful a tie had to be consummated and, with the inheritance secured for her sons, Pudentilla broke off with Clarus and wrote to her elder son that she now wished to make a suitable second marriage. So Pontianus, fearing that a selfish step-father might divert his mother's property from himself and Pudens, hastened home to take an active part in the family crisis. At Oea he found Apuleius ill, and in the name of old intimacy and with an unexpressed hope, begged him to move from the

house of his friends, the Appii, to his own home.
There Apuleius passed a year of convalescence,
assisting in the education of the two young men
and learning Pudentilla's sterling qualities. At
the end of the year, now restored to health, he
gave a public lecture which was such a brilliant
success that Pontianus seized the moment of
the afterglow to propose that he should marry
his mother and remain in enthusiastic Oea.
Although lukewarm at first because he wished
to travel and because the lady was considerably
older than himself (over forty), Apuleius soon
accepted the idea owing to Pudentilla's virtues,
and the marriage ceremony took place in a
country villa. This, Apuleius says in his trial,
was to save the expense of an elaborate wedding, but it may have been because of family
difficulties that had already arisen.

Pontianus had cooled toward Apuleius after
his own marriage, under the influence of his
wife's father, Herennius Rufinus, but had apolo-
gized for his conduct. Before, however, he
could act as a reconciler in the family relations
Pontianus died. This gave Rufinus and the relatives of Pudentilla's first husband a chance to
work upon the young and susceptible Pudens.
Aiming at Pudentilla's fortune, they brought

suit through Pudens against Apuleius, first for murdering Pontianus, a charge which he challenged so instantly that they dropped it, and then for having won Pudentilla's affections by the use of magic.

Apuleius acting as his own lawyer had a chance to tell the court and posterity what he thought of his wife's relatives and he made rich use of it. The trial was held at Sabrata (about forty miles west of Oea), where the proconsul Claudius Maximus was holding court. Apuleius' scintillating and humorous speech of defense will be studied later, but here is the time to review his character-sketches of his accusers. Declaring that the property is the one real cause of their attack, he shows up the old scoundrels, Sicinius Aemilianus, Pudentilla's brother-in-law, and Herennius Rufinus, the father-in-law of Pontianus, in their true colors, and then paints no less vividly that precocious young criminal, his step-son Pudens, governed by lust, depraved enough to malign his own mother and bruit false rumors publicly through the forum about her marital relations. The description of the vulgarity, illiteracy and venality of these persons is anything but pleasant reading, but seems to bear the stamp of veracity.

Most of the charges made by the plaintiffs were trivial or fictitious so that Apuleius was able to sweep them away by humor and sarcasm and to win the belief of his hearers and readers when he affirmed that the root of the whole trial was not horror of magic but envy of property. The attention which Apuleius paid to this aspect of the case demands consideration. First he admitted his own poverty, glorying in being a poor philosopher, and showed that he had once had an adequate fortune, but had voluntarily diminished his patrimony by expenditures for education and travel, and by gifts to friends. Next he described how Pudentilla's father-in-law had tried to keep her property in the family by forcing her engagement to one of his sons who was both boorish and decrepit. He portrayed his wife's sense of business responsibility: in keeping her property intact during her long widowhood, in securing her father-in-law's property for her sons, in inspecting the accounts of her stewards, shepherds and grooms; in planning a quiet wedding with Apuleius in the country to avoid the expenses of presents to the populace and dinners to the family, such as she had incurred to the amount of 50,000 sesterces when Pontianus was mar-

ried. Then he showed that, supported by his
own wishes, she had not neglected the interests
of her sons at the time of this second marriage,
for she had bestowed upon Apuleius only a
moderate dowry (300,000 sesterces) with the
condition that this should revert to Pontianus
and Pudens in case she bore Apuleius no children; in case she did, it should be divided
among the children of her two husbands. Later,
after Pudens had shown himself corrupt, irre-
sponsible and unfilial, she had wished to disin-
herit him, but Apuleius had insisted on her
making Pudens her heir and leaving himself
only a small inheritance. And finally, he was
not spending her money: it was Pudentilla herself who had bought a small farm in her own
name for 60,000 sesterces. So Apuleius cleared
himself from the charge of having married
Pudentilla for her wealth.

The charge of having used magic arts was
more difficult to face, for as Apuleius com-
mented, no accusation is easier to make, or
more difficult to refute. Apuleius' sophistry is
so elaborately subtle that at one moment he
gives the impression that he would be proud to
be numbered among the great magicians of the
world and the next shows carefully that there

is no evidence against him to prove that he practised magic. We wonder, even as we read, whether he was actually acquitted or whether the case was dismissed as unproved. We know that he went on with his career as lecturer afterwards, but he left Oea for Carthage, finding himself perhaps too notorious in Pudentilla's home.

At Carthage, his brilliant discourses, his amazing fluency in both Greek and Latin, his scintillation in those extempore displays which were part of the sophist's art won him so great a reputation that statues were erected to him and he was made priest of Aesculapius, an office of great dignity and prestige, during the holding of which he gave gladiatorial games to the people. The only certain date in his life is fixed by one of these speeches, the panegyric on Scipio Orfitus (*Flor.* 17), which must have been delivered in 163 A.D. Another speech (*Flor.* 9) is less exactly placed by a reference to the "Caesars" which sets it in the joint rule of Marcus Aurelius and Lucius Verus, 161–169 A.D. Probably in the last part of his life Apuleius was interested no less in philosophy than in rhetoric and wrote his translations and adaptations of some of the Platonic writings.

We do not know the date or place of his death, but we must picture these years in Carthage as comfortable, sustained by Pudentilla's fortune, stimulated by the plaudits of great audiences, enriched by the eternal quest for knowledge on which his active spirit travelled after marriage had restricted his corporeal peregrinations.

It is difficult to visualize this magnetic Roman, for the contorniate published by Bernoulli is probably fictitious and his own descriptions of himself are utterly contradictory: now he is the unkempt philosopher, haggard, lean, with matted hair; now a desirable *parti* for a widow of forty, a youth not to be despised for body, spirit or fortune; again a priest of the Egyptian goddess Isis, one of the Pastophori, stalking about Rome with shaven head and clad in linen stole. A Protean figure! But yet the color and perfume of his personality may strike our senses from his works.

# III. THE WRITINGS OF APULEIUS

## I. The Metamorphoses

" That I to thee some joyous jests may show in gentle glose
And frankly feed thy bended ears with passing pleasant prose:
So that thou deign in seemly sort this wanton book to view,
That is set out and garnished fine, with written phrases new,
I will declare how one by hap his human figure lost,
And how in brutish formed shape his loathed life he tossed,
And how he was in course of time from such estate unfold,
Who eftsoons turned to pristine shape, his lot unlucky told." [3]

APULEIUS' permanent fame rests not on his being a brilliant sophist, a revered magician, or a holy priest of Isis. His novel is what gives him his unique place in the assemblage of great Latin writers. The history of ancient fiction has yet to be written on the basis of the discoveries of papyri which redate the extant Greek romances, but to understand Apuleius' achievement it is necessary to recall a few facts about the development of the prose romance.

In the history of Roman literature we are confronted with two stories, the *Satyricon*, written by Petronius, probably Petronius Arbiter of the time of Nero, and the *Metamorphoses* of

Apuleius, which are unique, brilliant and mature productions. They are utterly different in scene, subject, characters, treatment, form and state of preservation. The *Satyricon* is laid in Southern Italy, the *Metamorphoses* in Greece (particularly Thessaly) and Rome. The subject of the *Satyricon* may be the wrath of the offended god, Priapus, but is more largely centered on realistic scenes of low life as the principal characters are freedmen and slaves. The *Metamorphoses* deals with the experiences of an intellectual, supremely interested in magic, folk-lore and religion, and might almost be called the "Odyssey" of Lucius' Soul or an ancient "Pilgrim's Progress." Through the *Satyricon* runs a satyric vein of laughter at pretentious freedmen, bombastic poets, tedious rhetoricians, sensual women. The language of the narrative is crisp and colloquial. The *Metamorphoses* is romantic in tone; it treats even the most extravagant episodes seriously; the language is artificial, polished and in parts elaborated with all the skill of the rhetorician's art. The *Satyricon* is written partly in prose, partly in verse, following as its title suggests the Varro or Menippean type of Roman *satura*, which was a medley in both content and form.

[ 38 ]

CUPID AND PSYCHE
The Capitoline Group

The *Metamorphoses* is entirely in prose and
for this reason as well as for the fact that Apuleius admits his debt to a Greek story seems
more closely akin to the Greek romances than
to Petronius' work.

One great difficulty in comparing the scope
of these two works is that the *Satyricon* is a
fragment, only two books and those incomplete
out of possibly sixteen in the original, while
Apuleius' whole composition is before us. From
the two stories as they stand, however, their
whole conception and treatment is seen to be
very different. Their common elements are tales
of adventure and of love. Petronius' book is
more Roman for the Romans, and to my mind,
belonging in the development of satire, rather
than of the novel, completes the justification of
Quintilian's claim that in the history of literature satire was the peculiar contribution of the
Romans.

Apuleius' *Metamorphoses* may stand to us at
least as the first complete Roman novel extant.
It was in his time, the second century A.D., that
the Greek prose romances were also developing
apace, and Greek novels like " Chaereas and
Callirhoe " and " Habrocomas and Anthea "
were being produced. Of course, stories had

been told all down through the history of
Greece, but first in poetry: the minstrel's lay,
the epic narrative, the dramatic narrative of
messenger's speech in tragedy, love-stories
hinted in passionate lyrics and elegiacs, wrought
into Euripidean tragedy or travestied in the
New Comedy, rendered idyllic in the late
pastorals. The prose story, beginning in animal
fables and old wives' tales told to children by
the fire, seeps into prose writing in Herodotus'
history in the form of both adventure and romance, appears almost full-grown in Xenophon's *Cyropaedia* in the tale of Abradatas and
Panthea, becomes an exercise in the schools of
the rhetoricians, finally under Oriental influence
gains an identity of its own in the shape of the
short story in prose, then the novel.

The Romans knew the *novelle* in the first
century B.C., for Ovid says that the Roman historian Sisenna translated Aristides, the author
of the *Milesiaca* or Milesian Tales, into Latin,
and Plutarch tells us how the Parthian Surena
was horrified after his victory over Crassus at
Carrhae by finding in the knapsack of one of
the Roman officers Aristides' ribald stories. The
character of these stories was frivolous, amusing, often erotic, generally indecent, hence

Surena's criticism and the later Puritanical comment of the Emperor Severus on his defeated rival Albinus that he had grown old over the study of Milesian tales.

From the first century B.C., also comes the collection of Love Romances of Parthenius, short accounts in Greek prose written by an elegiac poet of Nicaea, dedicated to Cornelius Gallus and offered to him as embryo stories to be expanded in epic or elegiac poetry. These miniature romances, which were gathered by Parthenius from many writers, are largely mythological and imaginary, deal chiefly with unhappy love, and were selected apparently as unfamiliar stories with an appeal to the imagination which could make them useful for a poet's emotional treatment. How Gallus might have used them is suggested by Ovid's *Heroides*, imaginary love-letters of mythological heroines, written in elegiac verse. These constitute a special type of romantic short story.

That the longer Greek romances were known certainly in the early part of the first century A.D. is proved by the Ninus-story found on an Egyptian papyrus. In fact the evidence of the papyri has helped to re-date the extant Greek novels so that several are placed in the second century of our era.[4] When, therefore, Apuleius wrote his *Metamorphoses* the Greek short story had developed and been translated into Latin; the writing of Greek novels had begun and was flourishing; and in Latin the Varro type of satire in Petronius' *Satyricon* had created a peculiarly Roman form of quasi-fiction. It is clear that Apuleius did not invent this form of literature. He was simply a vital part of a story-telling age. Probably not even his particular plot was original. Nevertheless he showed unique genius in the composition of his novel.

It is reasonable to begin the consideration of Apuleius' writings with the *Metamorphoses* not only because it is his greatest work, but because it may have been his first in point of time. It is uncertain in what order Apuleius' works were produced and published. The approximate date of the *Apologia* has been carefully and logically estimated by Erwin Rohde as about 158 A.D., but whether the *Metamorphoses* and the *Florida* were written before or after the *Apologia* cannot be conclusively demonstrated. It seems probable that the *Florida* were written afterwards, as their facile brilliancy of delivery presupposes long practice in the sophist's art and the known dates in them fall in the reign of

Marcus Aurelius and Lucius Verus. As for the *Metamorphoses,* scholars are almost equally divided as to whether it preceded or followed the *Apologia.* Those who maintain that it preceded claim that *per se* it is a work of youth, romantic and often frivolous; that internal evidence shows that it was written in Rome for the Romans and that as far as is known Apuleius spent only his young manhood in Rome. Those who believe that it was written after the *Apologia,* declare that since it is full of references to the art of magic, some mention of it, had it been known, would certainly have been made by Apuleius' accusers in his trial for magic and answered by him in the *Apologia,* which is not the case. In answer to this it may be said that according to the manuscript tradition the *Metamorphoses* was not published under the name of Apuleius; that if the book was brought out in Rome, it may not have been known in Africa; that as it was a romance, the plaintiffs may not have considered it convincing evidence for their attack; or they may have referred to it, and Apuleius may not have replied to that point. None of these arguments is conclusive, but as the balance of probability seems to me on the side of early publication I am going to take up first the *Golden Ass,* as later readers lovingly or derisively termed this great story.

The plot is simple, for the thread on which are strung many disconnected short stories is the narrative of the life of Lucius, the hero, who by dabbling in magic was transformed into an ass; his many adventures in that shape until he could secure the antidote, a meal of roses; and finally his re-transformation through the aid of the Egyptian goddess Isis. The story is told by Lucius in the first person. Notable as its bizarre and romantic character, is the feeling for animals that it contains: their weariness and miseries, their stupidities and helplessness, their mistreatment and suffering at the hands of men. And from the plot also the grotesque and the humorous are not lacking. Lucius, the Ass, is a very observant and amusing Four-footed.

The individual stories loosely grouped around this central plot may be classified according to their general character as stories of the horrible, the laughable, the mysterious and the mystic. Or they may be classified more specifically on the basis of their subjects: stories of magic, including the Murder of Socrates by the Witch Hypata, How Pamphile became an Owl, the Watching of a Corpse, or

How Thelyphron lost his Nose; stories of crime, including Three Robber Stories, the Dragon's Cave, Torture by Ants, Three Sons Dead, The Woman who murdered Five; love-stories, some of them comedies, The Lover and the Tub, the *Amante* who Sneezed, the Sandals under the Bed, some tragedies, The Bride Charite, the Murder of a Stepson, and the fairy-story of Cupid and Psyche; stories of pure adventure, like Lucius' Fight with Three Brave Wine-skins; and stories finally of religion, or the supernatural, the Assyrian Fortune-Teller, the Egyptian who raised the Dead, the Debaucheries of Syrian Priests, Goddess Isis and her Worship. Of course, in any such classification, the divisions overlap and certain tales belong in two or more categories.

No list of titles can suggest the kaleidoscopic changes of subject and tone in this story as it rushes from murder to marriage, from robber's cave to heaven's high throne, from the magic spells of filthy witches to the mystic vision of great deity, from the obscenities of vulgar immorality to the bodiless rapture of spiritual trance. The fascination of its startling varieties is enhanced by the multiform expression, the style varying with theme and mood. Now the

braying of the ass is heard, now the shriek of
captured bride. Now hilarity bursts forth in
unrestrained laughter at the festival of the
Comic Spirit, Risus; now rise the dulcet
voices of the Muses singing Psyche's wedding-
hymn.

Even the sampling of this delicious farrago
raises the question: where did Apuleius get the
ideas for his main plot and for his various
stories? In the first chapter of the *Metamorphoses* he gives two clues to his sources: the
story is a Milesian narrative; it is a Greek
story. Among the writings of Lucian there exists a Greek tale with the title Λούκιος ἢ ὄνος,
"Lucius or the Ass," which in much briefer
form has the same general plot as the *Metamorphoses* but a different ending, as the hero
regains the shape of man at an obscene exhibition, and the influence of Isis through vision,
prayer, pageants, priests and initiation has no
part in this Lucius' re-transformation. Another
Greek version of the same story is known from a
reference in Photius to the *Metamorphoses* of
Lucius of Patrae. (Bibl. cod. 129, Migne)
Scholars have not finished discussing what is
the interrelation of these three versions of the
Lucius-story, and different theories have been

advanced as that Λούκιος ἢ ὄνος was the original version which Apuleius followed; or that Apuleius wrote both the Greek and the Latin *Metamorphoses,* while another Greek writer made an epitome of them in Λούκιος ἢ ὄνος. Careful study of the text of the two extant versions and of Photius' description of the third that is lost, has gone far toward proving that the two stories which we have both go back to a common source, the lost *Metamorphoses* of Lucius of Patrae. The comparative work of a recent dissertation by B. E. Perry makes it seem plausible that Lucian wrote that lost story of which Λούκιος ἢ ὄνος is an abridgement by another hand, and that this was the source of Apuleius' tale. Where Lucian or some anonymous Greek author found his material is another question.

The Milesian element in the novel is different. The name, as we have seen, comes from the work of Aristides, who in the second century B.C. wrote a book of stories laid in or around Miletus and hence called Μιλησιακά· These stories, which were erotic and openly indecent, were extremely popular. From them the name Milesian came to be given to stories which were light, entertaining, usually erotic, often scandalous. Many of the separate tales in Apuleius' novel are of this character.

How original Apuleius' work is can be judged only partially and formally from a comparison of his work with the Pseudo-Lucian's and a study of the elements common to both, or from a study of the stories in Apuleius which are essential to the main plot and so probably in his prototype, and of the stories which may well be additions because they do not depend upon the main plot at all, or have only some loose connection. His originality is felt more in the weaving of the whole fabric; so richly colored and lifelike is this tapestry of cunning witches, amorous women, deceived husbands, maltreated slaves, corrupt priests, valiant robbers, injured beauties, good physicians, bad small boys, sneaking weasel, white horse, ass betrayed by shadow, Psyche the beloved of the Love-God, the Olympian deities, finally pageant and pomp of processions in honor of Isis, the Mother of the Myriad Names. The man who composed this novel was fired with love of adventure, of excitement, of romance, of mystery, of magic and of mysticism; he was entertained by life as he would fain have his Gentle Reader entertained by his writing.

For out from behind the long-eared, long-nosed mask of the ass peers not only the hero Lucius, but Apuleius himself. Hide-and-seek through the book he plays with his Reader, for in the first chapter the writer seems to be speaking of himself when he says that he learned to write Latin at Rome under no teacher, but with much labor, and his style must still have some flavor of his forensic toil. The whole book was written at Rome and for the Romans, as many allusions testify (to the *metae Murciae,* VI. 8; to the Roman marriage laws, VI. 22; to the fines for being late at the Senate, VI. 23; to the law about slaves, VI. 4; to Caesar, XI. 17). And in the last Book, the Eleventh, by a slip or a confession, hero Lucius becomes the man of Madaura instead of from Corinth; moreover, his residence in Rome and his repeated religious initiations correspond to the facts of Apuleius' life as set forth by himself in his autobiographical oration. The eleventh book in its amazing spiritual confession might form a chapter in William James' *Varieties of Religious Experience* as an illustration of a sincere autobiographical account of conversion; and this probably represents Apuleius' own religious history.

The gem of the whole book is the story of Cupid and Psyche, a creation of such delicate lustre that it shines like a pearl amid the multicolored bits of glass in the mosaic of the other tales. The story is told in the robbers' cave, by an old hag who cooks for them, to the young bride Charite whom they have carried off, to divert her mind from terrors while she waits for her parents to ransom her. "An old wives' tale" the aged crone calls it, and it begins in the good old-fashioned way:

> Once in a city of old
>   Lived a king and a queen.
>     These had three fair daughters,
>       But the fairest of all was the third.[5]

All the marks of a folk-lore tale appear in the story: beautiful, neglected princess, marriage to a husband whom she must not see, jealous elder sisters, disappearance of husband when this prohibition is neglected, jealousy of husband's mother who sets the bride dangerous and cruel tasks, accomplishment of tasks by supernatural aid, final re-union of bride and husband. Such stories, as Andrew Lang has shown, appear among all nations, not merely in the Indo-European.

Strangely enough, however, there is no trace of the story in Greek and Latin literature until it appears in Apuleius' perfect form in the second century A.D. And here hero and heroine have received the names Cupid and Psyche, Love and the Soul. Many are the conjectures as to whether Apuleius had before him some lost Greek story, or whether with real genius, from his reading of the Platonic writings, he saw how by fitting the names Cupid and Psyche to the lovers in the folk-tales he could lift the simple fairy-story to the spacious halls of the Olympians and enwrap it in all the glamour of the old Greek philosophy. For it is Venus herself who is the jealous mother-in-law, and she and the other dwellers on Olympus are treated with all the gentle satire of the Lucianic dialogues.

But while it is the Queen of Love who sets her daughter-in-law the cruel tasks of sorting grain, of fetching flock of golden fleece, of bringing water from the Styx, of entering Hell and carrying forth a box of Proserpine's fair charm, young Psyche, just as in fairy folk-tales, is aided in supernatural ways and by creatures of the earth: by busy ants, by vocal reed, by mighty eagle, by talking tower. And woven through this startling combination of the Greek

deities and nature's humblest servants is a delicate thread of haunting allegory. Is this the
eternal story of Love and the Soul? If not,
why are Venus' servants named Anxiety and
Sorrow? Why is her enemy dubbed Sobriety,
and why is the child of Love and the Soul called
Joy? From the Latin writer Fulgentius in the
sixth century down to our own time an elaborate allegorical interpretation has again and
again been given to the whole story, inevitably
with many variations.

Probably, I think, when Apuleius imprisoned
once for all what Walter Pater beautifully
called " the floating star-matter of many a delightful old story," he chose to clothe his old
wives' tale not only in the gorgeous robes of
Greek mythology but to cast an almost invisible veil of philosophical mysticism over the
face of this

> *Latest born and loveliest vision far*
> *Of all Olympus' faded hierarchy.*

No other part of Apuleius' work has had so
great influence in literature and art as this
story.

The other unique feature of Apuleius' *Metamorphoses* is the picture of the worship of Isis

in the final Book. No other document from antiquity gives us so full an account of the ceremonies and mysteries of the Egyptian goddess, nothing else explains so fully the hold which her cult had upon her votaries. An outline may show how varied is the material.

When Lucius, the Ass, escaping from an obscene exhibition, came to Cenchreae near Corinth, he went to sleep on the seashore, then awaking in the dead of night when the full moon was shining on the water, he offered prayer to the queen of heaven, begging her aid and delivery. When again he slept, lo! from the sea rose the goddess herself in all her majesty (the description is marvellous) and deigned to speak an answer to his prayer, first telling him that she is the great mother of all the world, worshipped under many names, then promising him help at her spring festival of the launching of the sacred boat. Then followed the pageant of the festival with all its masqueraders, the musicians, the initiates in white, the priests with sacred light and relics, then the gods themselves, among them, Anubis, the dog-headed, the sacred symbols of deity, the holy vessel. Finally the appointed priest offered the Ass a garland of roses and slowly he resumed the shape of man, received the benediction of the priest, joined the procession to the shore for the launching of the Sacred Boat which opened spring navigation, then returned to the Temple for the prayer of blessing on Emperor, Senate, knights and all the Roman people.

Lucius' great day was ended, but he could not return to normal life again even though his relatives came to aid him. His mind was too full of gratitude to his saviour-goddess and desire for her worship, and night after night he had repeated visions of Isis who always bade him be initiated in her rites, until he longed for nothing so much. A final vision announced that the appointed time had come. Under the direction of the priest, Mithras, Lucius listened to mystic words in the temple, took lustral baths, fasted ten days, and finally, clad in a linen robe, he was taken at night alone to the most sacred part of the temple, where his initiation was completed. His own words may describe his experience:

" I approached the borderland of death, trod the threshold of Proserpina, was borne through all the elements and returned; at midnight I saw the sun shining with a brilliant light; I approached the gods of the nether and the upper world and adored them in person near at hand."

Whatever this experience was, it was in no normal state that Lucius came out from it, and his exaltation was not yet over, for clad in a mystic robe, a lighted torch in his hand, crowned with flowers, he was exhibited upon a pedestal like the sun god himself to all the people who gathered to see him, and for three days banquets and ceremonies followed. At the end he fell prostrate at the feet of the goddess, weeping, praying, consecrating himself to her service. Soon after, going to Rome, he continued his worship at the Temple of Isis in the Campus Martius and twice again by visions he was directed to be initiated in the ceremonies of Osiris, and each time, though the expense was great for this *poor man of Madaura* he obeyed and finally became one of the Pastophori or high priests, and under the blessing of Osiris prospered greatly as an advocate in the Forum. Here the *Metamorphoses* ends.

Even so slight a narrative of this great Eleventh Book may show how remarkable an account it gives of personal religious experience. There are two types of interpretation of the meaning of Apuleius' account of his first initiation and of what actually happened to him. One set of commentators believes that through the skill of the priests various phenomena were produced (for example, the light of the sun by the flash of torches), that the priests themselves enacted a drama of the gods' lives, or that colossal figures of the gods were cleverly manipulated or symbols of them suddenly presented to stimulate the imagination. That is, this interpretation tries to find material causes for each sensation.

The other type of interpretation, represented by de Jong's work, seeks to show that the experiences described would easily come about in the psychological state produced by fasting, continence, the awe of night, inner shrine, loneliness, and that in such an ecstatic sleep or trance, the initiate seemed to himself to descend into death, to enter the door of Hell, to go through not only the earth, but fire, air, water — all the elements — to see a great light and finally to behold the apparitions of the gods. Both the ancients and Christian writers recognized this experience of religious ecstasy and its possibilities. De Jong points out that magic arts and mysteries had much in common; in both the same effects were produced; and that probably the secret in all mysteries, as in the Eleusinian, lay in the use of magic formulae. These were used in the Egyptian cults and it is clear from writers on magic, from the magic papyri, from Roman writers like Porphyrius and even from Apuleius himself that Egyptian priests used magic. It must be remembered that the priest Mithras read much to Lucius out of a mystic book in preparation for the initiation. With his mind carefully prepared by these words hidden from the curious reading of the profane, in the state of exaltation produced by dreams, fasting, continence and night, Lucius succumbed to that cateleptic state in which his subconscious mind worked over material already suggested to it, and underwent not merely the enthusiasm of the lesser religious experience, but the complete ecstasy of final revelation. So Lucius found his freedom.

It is possible to find in the whole *Metamorphoses* a half-hidden allegory, a sort of Roman Pilgrim's Progress, in which Everyman, experimenting with life and its occult possibilities, caught in the animal body of his own lasciviousness, wanders through life, not a little lower than the angels, but a little higher than the beasts, dabbles in magic, observes all varieties of religious experiences and hears the true story of Love and the Soul, finally is saved by the roses of rapt faith in ecstatic worship of God, one deity in myriad forms. But this seems to interpret too curiously. Rather the *Metamorphoses* turns the pages of life itself and without particular propaganda or purpose shows a restless age, tired of megalomania and empire, craving new sensations, demanding to be startled into attention, to be entertained by the marvellous, and to be transported by magic or religion beyond the ennui and satiety of everyday to glimpses of a supernatural world.

## 2. THE APOLOGIA

THE *Apologia* in many ways is not so baffling a literary work as the *Metamorphoses*. Certain definite facts about it are known. It was delivered when the proconsul, Claudius Maximus (about 156–8 A.D.), was holding court at Sabrata. Apuleius had gone there to act as his wife's lawyer in a case brought against her by the brothers Granii. He was suddenly accused by Sicinius Aemilianus, his wife's brother-in-law, of having murdered his step-son, Pontianus, and won his rich wife, Pudentilla, by

THE WRITINGS OF APULEIUS

magic arts. While the first charge was quickly dropped, in four or five days Aemilianus, on behalf of Apuleius' younger stepson Pudens, actually brought suit against Apuleius on the second indictment. Apuleius defended himself before Claudius Maximus in the speech called *Apologia* or *de magia*.

Although the work rests on such a foundation of fact, it is full of surprises for the reader. In the first place, the Romancer, the Novelist, the Mystic of the *Metamorphoses* is here a very clever and experienced lawyer who deserved, as Norden has pointed out, the appellation *advocatus summus et in iudiciis exercitatissimus,* "a very great advocate, with wide experience in the courts." This pleader, to be sure, does not forget nor lay aside the sophist's skill; indeed uses all his rhetorical powers for the refutation of various trivial charges presented by his adversaries and for certain brilliant digressions, splendid "purple patches," designed to hypnotize and conciliate the court-room. But the structure of the argument is clear, logical and forceful, and as cat with mouse, Apuleius plays with his adversaries, with velvet paws, raps of claws, before he snaps teeth on neck at end. The most convincing evidence and argument are reserved for a final climax that seems absolutely damnatory to the other side, and there the rhetoric of the sophist is swept away by the cold analysis of the legal evidence.

This logical and forceful construction of the speech is not on first reading its most conspicuous feature. To one accustomed to the dignified, serious, sonorous movement of Cicero's periods, the light humor, the laughing irony, the eloquent digressions, the gossiping account of family relations seem ill-fitted to a Roman court-room. Critics have indeed maintained that the speech was never given in this form, but re-written after delivery for literary circulation, but it seems reasonable to believe that under the development of the sophist's art juridical oratory may well have been considerably modified. The ancients themselves had distinguished the Attic and the Asianic style of oratory and writing: the purist's simplicity and stateliness; the entertainer's elaborations, antitheses, exuberances, bombast. That Asianism of which Apuleius in *Metamorphoses* and *Florida* is so complete an illustration could not but tinge the style of his forensic pleading. Yet under all its embellishments Norden finds the

*Apologia* a very mine of lore for the study of Roman jurisprudence.

The speech also gives an amazing revelation of private life in the period. The matter of inheritance and property has already been discussed in the account of Apuleius' life. No less illuminating is the side light thrown on the position of women in the province of Africa, on family relations, on the etiquette of the times, on education, on the prevalent interest and belief in magic. With Apuleius' other works, the *Apologia* stands as an unconscious revelation of everyday life in the time of the Antonines.

The outline of the speech is clear: an introduction which states the character of his accuser and explains why it is necessary to answer foolish charges lest he might seem by his silence to admit their truth; next the rebuttal of the minor accusations; finally a facing of the charge of practicing magic, both in the lesser instances presented by the plaintiff and in the main accusation of using the black art to win Pudentilla's hand.

Apuleius treats with easy humor the personal charges arraigned against him, of physical beauty, of writing poems on tooth-powder and love, of using a mirror, of being poor, and an-

swers each in the lightest way. As to personal
beauty, the court has only to look at him to
have the charge refuted. " Besides the fact that
I am of a commonplace appearance, my prolonged literary labors have wiped all charm
from my person, weakened my condition, dried
up the sap of life, obliterated my color, debili-
tated my vigor." The poem on tooth-powder he
recites willingly to show it was but a trifling
verse, sent with a present, and then he branches
off into a long discourse on cleanliness and the
care of the mouth in a mock-oratorical strain.
The charge of writing love-poetry he admits,
again quotes his effusions with relish, declares
that he is glad to be in the company of Plato
here, and in a brilliant paragraph tries to suggest to his Philistine opponents the mystic character of the divine Platonic love. Then he slips
from his beautiful solemnity to the merriest
ridicule of the charge that he had a mirror:
why, possession does not prove use; and if I
did look into a mirror, it were not sin to see
myself; or I may practice oratory before it as
Demosthenes did; or I may use it in my scientific experiments on rays of light; there are
many possibilities of defense. Then the last personal charge, of poverty, moves him to his great-

est eloquence. Poverty has long been the hand-maid of philosophy. Great possessions are but weights to the spirit. The standard of wealth is not in money or land, but in the soul of man, and the true philosopher cares for nought but wallet and staff.

After this introduction, Apuleius comes to the specific charges of his magical practices. His accusers said he had bought fish, dissected them and used them for magic; that he had made a slave fall down at his feet and also a woman; that he carried around a mysterious object concealed in a handkerchief; that he had raised a ghost at night; that he had had made a statuette of a horrible figure which he worshipped. To these charges again, his answers are easy: the fish he had dissected, but for nothing more magical than his scientific experiments; the slave-boy who had fallen at his feet was a miserable epileptic and so was the woman; the " mysterious object " was one of those revered symbols of the mysteries which all true Romans adore. Then the account of his having raised a ghost is the invented story of false witnesses; and the " horrible statuette " he displays to the court and lo! it is an exquisite figure of the god Mercury.

Next, with steady aim at cumulative climax, Apuleius approaches the final charges of having used magic to force Aemilia Pudentilla to marry him. The plaintiffs claim that before she met Apuleius, Pudentilla had no thought of new wedlock, but Apuleius shows that she had resolved on second marriage on the advice of her physician and was looking for a suitable person. They say also that she married at the age of sixty, which suggests coercion. This is libel, as the lady was only forty. " The marriage," they continue, " took place secretly in the country, a very suspicious circumstance." Apuleius retorts that Roman law has never pronounced country weddings illegal, and as a matter of fact they had a quiet wedding there to save the expense of an elaborate ceremony and of extravagant entertainment of their relatives. When his detractors at last bring forth their real grievance, that he married for money, he reminds them that on his own advice Pudentilla had already settled upon her sons a large portion of her fortune, that her dowry was small and held by him only in trust.

The most damning part of the accusation which Apuleius had to face was a letter to Pon-

tianus written by Pudentilla in which she herself said: "Apuleius has become a magician. I
have been bewitched by him and am in love."
To answer this, Apuleius simply demands that
the whole letter be read in court in order that
the context may show the original meaning of
Pudentilla's words:

"For when I was wishing to marry for the
reasons which I mentioned, you yourself persuaded me to choose him before all, since you
admired the man and desired to make him one
of our household through me. Now then when
malicious assailants of us are perverting your
thought, Apuleius has become a magician; I
have been bewitched by him and am in love.
Come, then, to me, while I am still in my
senses."

Probably the reading of this whole letter, by
showing how unprincipled the attack had been
and how illicitly the documents presented had
been used, undermined the whole accusation,
and made plausible Apuleius' counter-attack
that his accusers were really aiming at the possession of Pudentilla's fortune. By showing how
generous he had been in his financial dealings
with his stepsons, Apuleius cleared his honor,

before succinctly summarizing his arguments and eloquently appealing to the court to pronounce him innocent.

What the legal opinion of Claudius Maximus was is unknown. The older commentators believed that Apuleius was certainly acquitted. More recent critics point out that he never actually disproved some of the charges of experimenting in magic, that he professes admiration for the great magicians of the past, that he confesses owning a Mercury, who was a god worshipped as Psychopompos in magic rites, that the epileptic persons are never examined in court, that he shows an acquaintance with the use of boys for divination, that his general knowledge of magic is known from his other works. Certainly that knowledge cannot be denied, but Horace too as well as many other ancient authors wrote of magic rites without being accused of being wonder-workers. These critics point out also that Apuleius did not continue to reside in Oea and that Saint Augustine records that he made a speech about a proposed statue to himself in Oea, combating the opposition of the people of the town. But all this is inconclusive evidence, and it cannot be shown whether Claudius Maximus declared that the

case was unproved or Apuleius was acquitted of
the charges. In either event, his personal liberty
was unrestricted, for he appears next as a popular lecturer in Carthage, greatly admired and
richly honored.

### 3. THE FLORIDA

No popular lecturer in the United States
today has achieved greater fame than Apuleius
won from his declamations as he travelled from
city to city in Africa. This silver-tongued orator of little Madaura had a gift of eloquence
that brought all Carthage to his feet, made pro-
consuls propose statues to him and senates vote
honorary decrees. No one complete address of
his is extant, for the *Apologia* is forensic oratory, however much it savors of his rhetorical
training, but extracts from Apuleius' public
speeches were assembled in antiquity in a volume called *Florida* and these go far in showing
us the sophist's art and his own opinion of his
technique.

The name *Florida,* " Flowers," probably does
not refer to a blooming style, but to the fact
that various passages were culled from his discourses and made into one nosegay suggesting

the varied colors and scents of his many displays. Who made this collection is not known. As the passages are arranged in four books, there may have been an original collection of speeches in four books from which some unknown reader copied passages which appealed to him. Oudendorp believes them commonplaces which Apuleius had worked up for his impromptu speeches, but this theory is disproved by the fact that many of the selections are not *loci communes* but parts of orations on special occasions. Hildebrand thinks them excerpts taken down by stenographers, when the speeches were being delivered, but one wonders why stenographers should not record entire speeches. Krüger argues that Apuleius himself made a collection of pieces to illustrate his eloquence and hence called it *Florida,* but all are not of the exotic, flowery style. Rohde believes that Apuleius himself made the original collection of his oratorical works, part whole speeches, part selections, and then perhaps later another person worked over the whole, shortening it, but retaining Apuleius' own division of four books. In any case, whatever the original of the *Florida* was, here we have rich and varied illustration of the subjects and art by which Apuleius enthralled his audiences.

Before taking up these *Florida* it is well to consider for a moment how distinguished the profession of sophist was at this time. In his book, *The Universities of Ancient Greece,* J. W. H. Walden has vividly portrayed the sophist's education, emoluments and performances and has described how honored and honorable was their art in the second century. Emperors encouraged them, for Antoninus Pius gave honors and salaries to rhetoricians and philosophers throughout the provinces and he and Marcus Aurelius established endowed chairs at Athens not only for the schools of philosophy but also for the study of rhetoric, or sophistry. Moreover, the profession of the teacher, or philosopher, was given immunity from taxation and such public duties as aedileships, priesthoods, military service. Remuneration came either from salaries accompanying official appointments, paid by emperor or cities, or fees determined by the sophist himself and apportioned to the means of the student. Wealthy patrons like Herodes Atticus also made bountiful presents in recognition of the brilliant talents of individual sophists. Even greater than such pecuniary rewards were the honeyed applause of huge audiences, the statues and decrees that perpetuated the fame of golden words.

How technical a profession this sophistry was is only realized after reading ancient accounts of what was taught in the rhetoricians' schools. The students who came there had already passed through the elementary schools and through the schools of the grammarians, who taught the literature and the civilization of the Greeks and the Romans. The rhetorician trained the orator, and to do this he had to teach both the theoretical side by the study of the great orators and writers of the past, and the practical side in both the composition of every sort of speech and the art of delivery. Different forms of literature with their corresponding styles were both studied and practiced, and all the fine technique of words, sentence structure, orderly arrangement and appeal to audience as well as the method of delivery were made the subject of constant trial and searching criticism; and students were accustomed to be ready to make impromptu efforts on subjects suddenly proposed to them. The brilliant displays of the sophist's skill which intoxicated great audiences were produced after long, vigorous training, years of practice and the experiences of travel and knowledge of the world. All this helps explain what Apuleius says of his own art.

The subjects of the *Florida* are typical themes of the sophist's business: encomiums of great men and of great cities; anecdotes, both mythological and historical, and fables; scientific discourses along the lines of ethnography, geography, natural history; passages on the art of sophistry.

Three of those which refer to distinguished persons can be approximately dated and so have especial value for the life of Apuleius, as we have shown: Number 9, which by its reference to the favor of the Caesars must belong in the joint rule of Marcus Aurelius and Lucius Verus, 161–169; Number 16, which thanks Aemilianus for proposing a statue of Apuleius at Carthage, and refers to his coming proconsulship of Africa, which could not have been earlier than 166; Number 17, a panegyric on Scipio Orfitus, proconsul 163–164. Other distinguished men honored, besides living politicians, are Alexander the Great, Socrates, Thales, Antigenidas the flute-player, Philemon the Comedian. Stories told are "How Doctor Asclepiades restored a Dead Man"; "How the Cynic Crates wooed his Bride"; "How the Piper Marsyas contended with Glorious Apollo"; and the fable of Fox and Crow.

As illustrations of Apuleius' lost scientific works may be taken three fragments of quasi-scientific nature: accounts of the characteristics of the Indians, the topography of Samos, and the habits of the parrot. All these subjects suggest the range of interest in the *Florida,* but nothing of the method of treatment. The style in them is as varied as the themes.

There are several passages in which Apuleius talks about his technique and these are illuminating. Part of his account of his training has already been quoted in his Life, — the varied cups from which he had quaffed his education. At the end of that passage, he comments on the resultant range of his work. "Empedocles composed odes, Plato dialogues, Socrates hymns, Epicharmus melodies, Xenophon histories, Crates satires; your Apuleius cultivates all these and cherishes the Muses nine with equal devotion." Such vigorous training with professors of literature, rhetoric and philosophy Apuleius would have required of everyone who dared assume the name of philosopher, and just as King Alexander forbade any likeness of himself to be made except by the supreme artists whom he selected, Apuleius would ordain that not everyone should boldly simulate the rôle of philosopher. Then a few truly learned men might lead the life of contemplation and the inexperienced, the sordid, the ignorant might not imitate the philosophers by assuming their mien and basely counterfeiting their royal training. In this passage and others Apuleius shows that in his thought *philosophus* and *orator* are virtually one, and that to him as to Quintilian the true orator or sophist was the good man speaking, who governed his life by philosophical thought.

His sophist was not to have merely this mental training: tone of voice and diction were the indispensable means of communication which also must have their education. Thought and speech were the two faces of his Janus-like art. So Apuleius acknowledged to the audience that was listening to his panegyric on the proconsul Severianus: " The reputation I have acquired, your kind expectations do not permit any careless utterance, rather demand my most whole-souled work. For who of you would forgive me for one solecism? Who would grant me one syllable barbarously pronounced? Who would permit me to babble as madmen may ill-starred and ill-chosen words? Such language, to be sure, you easily and rightly forgive in others. But with me, every single word that I utter you examine keenly, you ponder on diligently, you test by file and plumb-line, you demand the polish of the lathe and the grandeur of the stage."

Such standards of both delivery and style Apuleius felt existent in the relation between his audience and himself; and part of his art, indeed of the technique of every sophist, arose from that consciousness of the audience that makes the great speaker play upon his hearers' thought and feeling as on the keys of his own finely tuned instrument. So Apuleius compliments the Carthaginians on the erudition of the throng assembled to hear him, and to make them *en rapport* with him declares that he is overwhelmed by speaking before his own people; his debt to them for education, for approval, for honors is so great that he cannot adequately re-imburse his fellow-citizens. " Yet always and everywhere I celebrate you as my parents, as my first teachers; again and again I try to repay my debt." Here he conciliates his audience. In another speech, he tells them that the success of his discourse depends on their response: "Now it rests with you to give favorable breeze to my swelling sails that they may not hang drooping, nor be reefed nor furled."

Again he urges the audience to judge his improvisations by a less severe standard than that which they apply to his finished written work, and declares that speaking extemporaneously on a subject suddenly proposed is like building a loose wall from rough stones, instead of laying quarried blocks, by rule and perpendicular. But the sophist must speak extempore if the audience wills, must even change from Greek to Latin in the midst of a discourse if that seems good to his hearers. And always he will attempt to satisfy them by a speech "strong in argument, sprinkled with epigrams, rich in illustration, abounding in eloquence."

Only the very language of Apuleius' discourses can illustrate by what wealth of ideas, of mood, of style he fulfilled his promises. Perhaps, however, I may venture to try to imitate in an English translation of the first fragment something of his subtle elaborations with all the alliterations, rhythms, rhymes, balanced antitheses and repetitions that make his style untranslatable.

"Pious travellers have the custom when some holy grot or sacred spot is seen by the roadside, to offer a vow, to proffer an apple, to tarry a while. So I on entering this holy of holiest cities, though I halt with no grace, must crave for indulgence, rave in refulgence, alter my pace. For no juster cause for pious delay may the wayfarer find in altar crowned with flowers or grotto decked with bowers or oak adorned with victims' heads, or beech adorned with victims' hides, or hillock hedged in awe or tree-trunk carved with saw or sod soaked with libations or stone drenched with potations. Little matters perhaps, ignored by those without wit, adored none the less by the few who seek what is fit."

## 4. PHILOSOPHICAL WORKS [6]

WHEN Saint Augustine [7] called Apuleius *Platonicus nobilis,* he was laboring under a stranger misconception than when he pronounced him a miracle-worker. Apuleius wrote about philosophy, but he was not a distinguished Platonist. The mental alertness and curiosity which had led him deep into the fields of science,

magic and religion turned his stylus also to the
realm of philosophical speculation to which his
studies in Athens must have introduced him. He
may perhaps have had three aims in his philosophical works: to make himself thoroughly
familiar with Greek philosophical thought by
the invaluable exercise of translation and re-
writing in another language; to convey to his
contemporaries the ideas of Plato and other
philosophers in an easier medium than the
original, just as Cicero had done; and third to
make in his speeches brilliant displays of great
learning along philosophical lines. To know
Apuleius it is necessary to understand the character of these writings. Few will read them, as
now no one would be aided by using Apuleius
as a door to Plato.

One work is really interesting, *de deo Socratis* " the God of Socrates," and as it links
with Apuleius' rhetorical writings it will be
studied first. It is an *oratio* as Apuleius calls it
(Chapter 4) and in it he is an *orator,* as he says
(Chapter 5), not a *philosophus*. His theme is
an old one, the doctrine of intermediary Spirits,
or Demons, mentioned by Hesiod, developed by
Pythagoras, acknowledged by Plato, recently
re-presented by Plutarch. Apuleius defines these

spirits as " in *genus* animal, in intellect rational, in feeling passive, in body aerial, in duration eternal," and says that they share the first three characteristics with men, the fourth is peculiar to themselves, and the fifth they have in common with the gods. Their nature makes them intermediary between gods and men, and their existence is proved by the need of such messengers and agents between deities and mortals. They convey the prayers and offerings of men to gods and work out the influence of gods on men. It is, moreover, these demons and not the gods (as poets, seeing only a half-truth, imagine) who are haters and lovers of men. For the celestial deities live in tranquillity, undisturbed by human passion, but the demons feel pity, indignation, anger, joy, in truth experience every phase of human emotion. There are different classes of these demons, and here Apuleius, adapting the Greek conception to Roman words, shows that the soul of man still in his body, his " Genius," as it was called in Roman nomenclature, is a demon, and so though of a different species are the Lemures, the wandering spirits of the dead, and the Lar Familiaris, the protective guardian of the family. But a higher, more august class of demons is composed of those spirits which have never been confined in the body, but have always been in charge of certain functions. Such are Sleep and Love. Such is the guardian spirit that watches over each man, and here belongs the demon of Socrates. That demon was only a warning voice, not an instigator to noble action, because Socrates himself was so perfect that he did not need exhortation. The oration is not merely expository, but contains fervid admonitions to Apuleius' hearers to devote themselves like Socrates to the study of philosophy and to the worship and care of their demons, since only so can they live happily.

Another work is a philosophical treatise in two books called *de Platone et eius dogmate,* " Plato and his Doctrine." Here are given short, popular abridgements of Plato's teachings, preceded by a somewhat fabulous account of the Master's life. Book I uses the *Timaeus,* Book II, the *Gorgias, Republic* and *Laws.* As Plato had divided philosophy into three parts, natural philosophy, ethics and dialectic, so apparently Apuleius planned to treat the subject in three books. In the first, he discusses the cosmos, dividing it into three principles: deity, the material world, the ideas. Next, the four elements which constitute the world (fire, water, earth, air) are discussed. An account follows of the World Soul, of time which is conditioned by the heavenly bodies, of the four groups into which created things fall, of the threefold order of the divinities, of the threefold division of the human soul. Only when the rational part has control is the soul sound. Only when soul and body work in harmony is man perfect.

The second book is dedicated to a *Faustinus filius,* but there is no evidence as to whether he was a real son of Apuleius or a spiritual son and disciple. The book deals with ethics according to Plato, and after a brief introduction about the virtues it discusses different classes of men, the excellent, the bad, and those who occupy a middle ground. Vice is not discussed, but virtue is, so also are rhetoric and the political life. Digressions follow on the general character of good and evil and remarks on friendship and love. Four classes of wicked men are then listed and the need of punishment for them is declared. After stating that among men the middle state is most common, he gives a picture of the perfect man, the one truly *sapiens:* self-reliant, secure, confident, disregarding the acci-

dents of life, taking misfortune without morose-
ness, believing that realities lie between him
and God, and that his spirit is immortal. Then
when the ideal philosopher has been depicted,
Plato's perfect and ideal republic is described
and after that the good state, which is more
adapted to the actual world.

The third book, on Dialectic, is lacking in
the manuscripts. A separate treatise called
περὶ ἑρμηνείας has been handed down under
the name of Apuleius, and as it deals with
formal logic, it was later added to these two
books on Plato's teachings. It is now generally
admitted that it was written by some later grammarian who wanted to supply the third book of
this work. The treatment is different, for in the
first two books the author professes to be following Plato and puts his thoughts in Plato's
mouth but in this monograph there is no
mention of Plato and the teachings are not
Platonic.

The writing of Apuleius called *de mundo* is a
translation of the Pseudo-Aristotelian περὶ
κόσμου, though Apuleius does not acknowledge
his debt. This work has had a strange literary
history. The Greek original was dedicated to an
Alexander, ἡγεμὼν ἄριστος, and this Alexan-

der came to be considered Alexander the Great and the writer, his teacher, Aristotle. But the content belied this, for the treatise is, according to Schanz, not Aristotelian, but rests on the Peripatetic teachings to which are added some Stoic elements, and Posidonius is also used; so the book is much later. The Alexander is probably Tiberius Julius Alexander, nephew of Philo, Procurator of Judaea 46–8 A.D., and Prefect of Egypt 66 A.D. When Apuleius worked over this book for the Romans, he dedicated this writing to " son Faustinus," as though it were his own, and when he mentions in it Aristotle and Theophrastus as sources he never refers to this Pseudo-Aristotelian περὶ κόσμου which he was virtually translating, nor to Aulus Gellius from whom he took the section on the winds. Yet the changes and additions which he made are but slight, some quotations from Latin poets, the insertion from Aulus Gellius, a few Roman expressions like " our sea " for the Mediterranean, a parenthesis on the grammarian's art, a reference to his own travels in Phrygia. At present this history of the book is more interesting to the average reader than its contents. For only a specialist working on the history of Roman variations of Greek philosophy would peruse carefully this combination of contemporary physical geography and pantheistic cosmology.

Among the lost works of Apuleius was a translation of Plato's *Phaedo,* another witness to Apuleius' interest in the great Idealist, and to the extent of his spiritual voyaging on the enchanted sea of the metaphysical. No account of Apuleius' mentality would be complete without a reference to other lost works that show the range of his interests and his talents: his poems, his Hymn to Aesculapius, his novel called "Hermagoras," his Epitome of History, his Orations, and the monstrous bulk of his scientific writing on *Quaestiones naturales,* treatises in both Greek and Latin on Fish, Trees, Agriculture, Music. He was voluminous and learned, apparently never wearied of the pursuit of knowledge already acquired, of the unknown and the unknowable, of the tangible and the hypothetical, of man and of God. With such widespread interests, his knowledge in any one line could not be intensive, but his culture was wide, and its breadth served what he undoubtedly perceived was his true function, that of a stylist who should develop new means for the communication of multiplex ideas in a complex age that needed for its surcharged life a more exuberant language.

Two summaries of his position in his world have impressed themselves on me. One is the incisive, epigrammatic summary in the *Encyclopedia Britannica:*

" His place in letters is accidentally more important than his genius strictly entitles him to hold. He is the only extant example in Latin literature of an accomplished sophist in the good sense of the term. The loss of other ancient romances has secured him a peculiar influence on modern fiction; while his chronological position in a transitional period renders him at once the evening star of the Platonic, and the morning star of the Neo-Platonic philosophy."

The other is Walter Pater's character sketch in *Marius the Epicurean,* for the sensitive hero who in boyhood one memorable day had read Apuleius' Golden Book with a poet friend, in manhood was invited out to a villa at Tusculum to a supper in honor of the great " literary ideal of his boyhood." There in the cool Alban hills amidst the quiet verities of peasant life, browsing cattle, eternal mountains, fashionable Rome had dined and been entertained by dances of young men representing brave warriors and the dying Paris, a famous reader had recited Lucian's account of Halcyon Days, and then the guest of honor loosed his own eloquence.

" The reader's well-turned periods seemed to stimulate, almost uncontrollably, the eloquent stirrings of the eminent man of letters then present. The impulse to speak masterfully was visible, before the recital was well over, in the moving lines about his mouth, by no means designed, as detractors were wont to say, simply to display the beauty of his teeth. One of the company, expert in his humours, made ready to transcribe what he would say, the sort of things of which a collection was then forming, the ' Florida ' or Flowers, so to call them, he was apt to let fall by the way — no *impromptu* ventures at random; but rather elaborate, carved ivories of speech, drawn, at length, out of the rich treasure-house of a memory stored with such, and as with a fine savour of old musk about them. Certainly in this case, as Marius thought, it was worth while to hear a charming writer speak. Discussing, quite in our modern way, the peculiarities of those suburban views, especially the sea-views, of which he was a professed lover, he was also every inch a priest of Aesculapius, patron god of Carthage. There was a piquancy

[ 85 ]

in his *rococo*, very African, and as it were per-
fumed personality, though he was now well-nigh
sixty years old, a mixture there of that sort of
Platonic spiritualism which can speak of the
soul of man as but a sojourner in the prison of
the body — a blending of that with such a relish
for merely bodily graces as availed to set the
fashion in matters of dress, deportment, accent,
and the like, nay! with something also which
reminded Marius of the vein of coarseness he
had found in the ' Golden Book.' All this made
the total impression he conveyed a very uncom-
mon one. Marius did not wonder, as he watched
him speaking, that people freely attributed to
him many of the marvellous adventures he had
recounted in that famous romance, over and
above the wildest version of his own actual
story — his extraordinary marriage, his religious initiations, his acts of mad generosity,
his trial as a sorcerer."

But this was not all. For as the guests separated, Marius, standing on the terrace and
looking across the Campagna to Rome, had a
chance " to converse intimately with Apuleius;
and in this moment of confidence the ' illumi-
nist,' himself with locks so carefully arranged,
and seemingly so full of affectations, almost like

one of those light women there, dropped a veil
as it were, and appeared, though still permitting
the play of a certain element of theatrical interest in his *bizarre* tenets, to be ready to explain
and defend his position reasonably. For a moment his fantastic foppishness and his preten-
sions to ideal vision seemed to fall into some in-
telligible congruity with each other. In truth,
it was the Platonic Idealism, as he conceived it,
which for him literally animated, and gave him
so lively an interest in, this world of the purely
outward aspects of men and things. Did material things, such things as they had had around
them all that evening, really need apology for
being there, to interest one, at all? Were not all
visible objects — the whole material world indeed, according to the consistent testimony of
philosophy in many forms — 'full of souls?'
embarrassed perhaps, partly imprisoned, but
still eloquent souls? Certainly, the contempla-
tive philosophy of Plato, with its figurative
imagery and apologue, its manifold aesthetic
colouring, its measured eloquence, its music for
the outward ear, had been, like Plato's old master himself, a two-sided or two-coloured thing.
Apuleius was a Platonist: only, for him, the
*Ideas* of Plato were no creatures of logical ab-

straction, but in very truth informing souls, in every type and variety of sensible things. Those noises in the house all supper-time, sounding through the tables and along the walls: — were they only startings in the old rafters, at the impact of the music and laughter; or rather importunities of the secondary selves, the true unseen selves, of the persons, nay! of the very things around, essaying to break through their frivolous, merely transitory surfaces, to remind one of abiding essentials beyond them, which might have their say, their judgment to give, by and by, when the shifting of the meats and drinks at life's table would be over? And was not this the true significance of the Platonic doctrine? — a hierarchy of divine beings, associating themselves with particular things and places, for the purpose of mediating between God and man — man, who does but need due attention on his part to become aware of his celestial company, filling the air about him, thick as motes in the sunbeam, for the glance of sympathetic intelligence he casts through it."

Pater makes Apuleius proceed to try on this new young friend part of his discourse on Demons and so eloquent was he that long afterwards Marius used "to hear once more that voice of genuine conviction pleading, from amidst a scene at best of eloquent frivolity, for so boldly mystical a view of man and his position in the world." For to Pater and his Marius, Apuleius was a real Platonist, however imperfectly he transmitted or illumined the master's visions. Perhaps each one of us according to our temperaments will find Apuleius most successful, most real as man, novelist, lawyer, sophist, philosopher, or literary artist.

# IV. APULEIUS IN THE MIDDLE AGES

## 1. IN THE EARLY MIDDLE AGES

THE varied fame which Apuleius attained in his life-time was surpassed by his post-mortem reputation. From the fourth century down through the Middle Ages his name was notorious and his work was the subject of discussion. Not even Virgil was regarded as a more powerful thaumaturge. Pagan and Christian writers alike recognized Apuleius as a magician. Philosophers responded to his mysticism. Story-tellers imitated his romance. Third-rate writers copied and debased his style. His lines of literary influence are as widely divergent as his own writings were antipodal. For to this same author may be traced accounts of mystic incubations and tales of risqué love affairs. From Saint Augustine to Boccaccio we find Apuleius casting his spells of one sort of magic or another over the imaginations of men and compelling attention and interest.

The history of the preservation of his works for us has two conspicuous landmarks: the oldest manuscript and the first edition. All the codices of the *Metamorphoses*, the *Apologia* and the *Florida* go back to a famous manuscript now in the Laurentian Library in Florence (*Cod. Laur.* 68.2) which contains also parts of Tacitus. This manuscript, which is written in Lombard characters and dates about the eleventh century, is believed to have been in the monastery at Monte Cassino and possibly through Boccaccio to have found its way to Florence. What is certain is that it goes back to an archetypal manuscript as old at least as the fourth century, for a subscription to the ninth book of the *Metamorphoses* shows that a certain Sallustius worked on it at that time. Poggio Bracciolini discovered the manuscript in 1427 in the possession of Nicolò de' Niccoli of Florence. This Niccoli bequeathed the treasure to the Convent of Saint Mark in Florence and from there it was transferred to the Laurentian Library. The extant manuscripts of the philosophical writings belong in general to the twelfth and thirteenth centuries, but one

(B of Brussels) was probably written in the beginning of the eleventh.

Interesting also is the history of the first edition of Apuleius' works. The first printing press in Italy was set up in 1465 at the Monastery of Subiaco in the Sabine Mountains by two Germans, Sweynheym and Pannartz. In 1467 they moved their press to Rome and there in 1469 (four years after printing was introduced into Italy) produced the *editio princeps* of Apuleius. The editor was Giovanni Andrea de Bussi, a pupil of the famous Vittorino da Feltre.

These are the most important links in the preservation of the text of Apuleius himself. Let us now ask what literary evidence there is of the knowledge of Apuleius down through the Empire, in the Dark Ages, in the Middle Years until the Renaissance. References to his writings appear in both grammarians and historians, and in the Christian Fathers. The earliest is in Lactantius, a professor of rhetoric who in the first part of the fourth century wrote a popular manual of the Christian doctrine. He refers to Apuleius in company with Apollonius of Tyana as a magician [8] and shows that he knew Apuleius' account of demons in the *de deo Socratis*.[9] Julius Capitolinus, an historian of Diocletian's

time, knew the *Metamorphoses*, for he wrote
that Clodius Albinus busied himself with old
wives' tales and grew senile over the Punic
Milesian stories of his Apuleius and literary
trifles.[10] Ausonius, the rhetorician, best known
by his *Mosella*, a poem in epic style, refers to
Apuleius in his *cento nuptialis* (a. 368), a
mosaic patched together out of lines and
phrases from Virgil. In the last part wherein he
describes with the most open wantonness the
*consummatio matrimonii*, he begs that no infer-
ence about his own life be drawn from his poetry and in self-justification asks his readers to
remember (referring to the *Apologia* IX) that
Apuleius was a philosopher in his life, but in his
epigrams a lover.

The story of Cupid and Psyche was imitated
about the beginning of the fifth century, by
Martianus Capella, who in northern Africa
wrote an encyclopaedia of the seven liberal arts
and to enliven his work introduced the arts at
the marriage of Philologia and Mercury. In
form his work was a *satura Menippea*, a mixture of prose and verse, but while the literary
type was taken from Varro, the setting and style
were both due to Apuleius, for the bride Philologia is wafted to Heaven, accompanied by the

songs of the Muses, and description and orna-
mentation recall Psyche's nuptials. The allego-
rizing treatment of the story of Cupid and
Psyche began in the sixth century with Fulgentius, the grammarian, who in his *Mythology*
gives a summary of the tale with a long allegorical explanation. Purser's translation of a few
lines of Fulgentius will show the curious involu-
tions of this and of all such allegorical interpretations: "They have considered that 'the
city' is as it were the World, and the King and
Queen to be God and Matter. To them they as-
sign three daughters, the Flesh, Spontaneity,
which we call Free Will, and the Soul —
Psyche in Greek means the Soul. . . . Venus,
that is Lust, envies her, and sends Desire to
work her ruin. But whereas Desire is both of the
good and of the bad, Desire falls in love with the
Soul, and mingles therewith in a kind of union
and persuades the Soul not to look upon his
face, that is, come to an understanding of the
delights of Desire." This is only the beginning
of Fulgentius' subtle exegesis.

Other secular writers of the fourth, fifth and
sixth centuries (Macrobius, Priscianus, Cassio-
dorus) mention Apuleius' name.

That the Christian Fathers knew Apuleius'

CUPID AND PSYCHE
By Rodin

writings is clear from the long discussions about
him in Augustine and from incidental references in such writers as Saint Jerome and Apol-
linaris Sidonius.[11] Carl Weyman's careful work
on style has shown that various patristic authors are indebted to Apuleius' diction and
phraseology for, as was natural, Tertullian of
Carthage (second and third centuries), Zeno of
Verona who was born in Africa (fourth century), Claudianus Mamertus of Vienna (fifth
century), all borrowed his language. The Arabic
Gospel of the Infancy although its source is
oriental has a strange parallel to Apuleius' Lucius in the story of a man transformed into a
mule who was restored by having the Christ
child placed upon his back. And the Pseudo-
Clementines, in the Latin version called "The
Recognitions," in its mixture of science and
magic, religion and romance, as well as in one
detail, seems to resemble closely the *Metamorphoses*. The extent of his influence and the
nature of his prestige are, however, manifested
most clearly in the writings of Saint Augustine.

In both his *Letters* and in *The City of God*,
Augustine shows himself thoroughly familiar
with Apuleius' "Golden Ass" (as he calls the
*Metamorphoses*), the *Apologia*, and the *de deo*

*Socratis.*[12] This was especially natural as he himself was born and educated in Africa and became Bishop of Hippo so that he had perhaps a covert pride in this fellow countryman whom he described as *Platonicus nobilis,* learned in both the Greek and the Latin tongues. He couples Apuleius of Madaura and Apollonius of Tyana as magicians and seems rather inclined to believe that they did perform miracles, but of course through the subtle aid of demons, not of angels; indeed, he is doubtful in his own mind as to whether Apuleius was actually transformed into an ass or invented the story of Lucius. He is horrified of course that the followers of Apuleius and Apollonius compare their miracles with those of Christ and he goes through long and persuasive arguments to show that Apuleius did not have much magical power: for all his magic he never attained any political office though he was clearly ambitious; moreover, he defended himself against the charge of magical practices " only wishing to show his innocence by denying such things as cannot be innocently committed." If he believed in magic he ought even to have suffered martyrdom for it. If he practiced magic, it must have been by the help of demons who, he himself admits, are constantly agitated and subject to anger. Such demons are therefore evil spirits and should not be used by good men as intermediaries between themselves and the gods.

Augustine's belief in evil spirits extends even to their power to hold intercourse with women. Since we have seen that Apuleius declared that the demons (not the gods) were lovers of women, indeed, that Love himself was a demon, it is possible to believe that Augustine took at least a part of this doctrine of incubation from Apuleius although in mentioning it he does not name him. "There is, too, a very general rumour," writes the Bishop,[13] "which many have verified by their own experience, or which trustworthy persons who have heard the experience of others corroborate, that sylvans and fauns, who are commonly called 'incubi,' had often made wicked assaults upon women, and satisfied their lust upon them; and that certain devils, called Duses by the Gauls, are constantly attempting and effecting this impurity is so generally affirmed, that it were impudent to deny it. From these assertions, indeed, I dare not determine whether there be some spirits embodied in an aerial substance . . . and who are capable of lust and of mingling sensibly with

women; but certainly I could by no means believe that God's holy angels could at that time
have so fallen."

This doctrine of incubation appears and re-
appears through the Middle Ages in more or
less distinct form. It lies half hidden in certain
stories of women tormented by devils. Gregory
the Great [14] tells of a nun who ate a lettuce leaf
in the garden and because she forgot to make
the sign of the cross over it, was straightway
seized by a devil. As soon as a priest, hastily
summoned, came to bring aid, the devil who had
seized her began to cry out from her mouth:
" What have I done? What have I done? I was
sitting by myself on a lettuce leaf; she came
and ate me." When the priest indignantly
ordered him to depart and not take possession of a maidservant of the omnipotent God,
off he went and never again had power to touch
her.

Bede [15] tells the story of Saint Juliana who
was beaten and horribly tortured by her father
and her betrothed, and then, when taken back
to prison, *had to contend openly with a devil;*
was again tortured on the wheel, in fire, by hot
oil, and finally beheaded. What tragic story of
hysteria and nocturnal visions might not mod-

ern psychology have discovered in these visitations of demons?

Isidore of Seville, like Augustine, believed that impure spirits, whom he calls demons, awake desire for illicit love, inspire passion, undergo various transformations and sometimes are even changed into the form of angels. This doctrine of incubation we shall find playing its part in the later Middle Ages in the writing of romance.

Such belief in the powers of darkness and their illimitable achievements is what made the church fathers, most of all the distinguished Augustine, credit in part Apuleius' potency as a magician and accept fully his theory of demons. The fact that Augustine himself gave such serious consideration to the reputation of Apuleius as a thaumaturge shows how notorious Apuleius' writings were in the early Middle Ages and how conspicuous his fame. Paul Monceaux has pointed out the significance of the controversies which were going on at this time over Apuleius' prestige:

" Au IVᵉ et au Vᵉ siècle, . . . les chrétiens, soutenus par l'autorité impériale et les magistrats, cherchaient à forcer les derniers retranchements du paganisme. Obligés par leurs dogmes mêmes de croire au merveilleux, ils admettaient la réalité des miracles d'Apulée et prenaient au sérieux les inventions de son roman; mais ils combattaient sa popularité avec d'autant plus d'acharnement. . . . Orateur et prêtre Apulée, aux yeux des Africains, avait le plus brillamment représenté l'ancienne civilisation au moment où les apôtres cherchaient à faire de Carthage une des capitales du christianisme. Adversaires et défenseurs personnifièrent en lui la société païenne. Les dieux vaincus avaient été relégués par les vainqueurs dans le cortège des diables: Apulée, leur prêtre et leur prophète, fut métamorphosé en sorcier. . . . Le succès de la légende s'explique par les luttes religieuses qui ont passionné l'Afrique romaine. Tous ont cru aux miracles d'Apulée: les païens l'ont opposé au Christ comme un grand thaumaturge; les chrétiens ont poursuivi en lui un sorcier et un antéchrist." [16]

In these early Middle Ages, from the fourth to the eighth century, Apuleius stands out most conspicuously as the magician, whose miracles were accredited alike by Christians and Pagans. But it must not be forgotten that in the fourth and fifth centuries he was known also as a writer of romance by Capitolinus, who despised his effeminating stories, by Martinanus Capella, who referred to the *Apologia* and perhaps imitated the tale of Cupid and Psyche in the marriage of Mercury and Philologia, and by Fulgentius Planciades, who allegorized the same tale.

## 2. IN THE MIDDLE AGES AFTER THE EIGHTH CENTURY

DID the Middle Ages after the eighth century know Apuleius? The answer to this query must be an emphatic " Yes," for scattered allusions, imitations, quotations show that from Byzantium to England there was some acquaintance with various works of the African. As early as the sixth century A.D., a statue of Apuleius had been erected at Byzantium, as the elegiacs of Cristodorus record.[17] And Psellus, the great Byzantine philosopher of the twelfth century, refers to Apuleius and his magic powers.[18] In Italy of the eleventh century Alphanus I of Salerno refers to *de deo Socratis*, but quotes a passage which is not in this or any other extant work of Apuleius. Certainly however the learned Bishop knew Apuleius' works.[19] Waifarius of Salerno also knew Apuleius, for he quotes the *Florida* (4, 18, 83), the one certain allusion to this work of Apuleius known in the early Middle Ages.[20] In the twelfth century Bernard Silvester of Tours based his work *On the Universe* on Apuleius' *De Mundo*. In England, Geoffrey of Monmouth (twelfth century) refers to the *de deo Socratis* and may possibly be indebted to Apuleius in his story of the birth of Merlin.[21] In the thirteenth century, Alexander Neckam repeated the fable of the crow and the fox as given in Apuleius' Prologus to *de deo Socratis* and Bartholemew of England used Apuleius' characterization of demons. (There is a twelfth century manuscript of the *de deo Socratis* in the British Museum, Harleian 3969.) Albertus Magnus, also, in discussing astrology refers to *de deo Socratis*. So widely diffused was some knowledge of Apuleius in the eleventh, twelfth and thirteenth centuries.

The work of Geoffrey of Monmouth raises an interesting question. Did Geoffrey know only the *de deo Socratis* or was he familiar also with the *Metamorphoses?* In the sixth book of his *Historia regum Britanniae* Geoffrey tells how a child of virgin birth was sought and the little Merlin proved to be such a one. His mother, Demetia, a princess who had been immured in

a convent, told the story of how a beautiful
youth appeared repeatedly in her cell at night,
wooed her, finally won her love and left her
with child. When the astonished king, her
father, consulted a magician to know if this
were possible, he was told by Maugantius that
the philosophers record many such incubations
and that Apuleius in his *de deo Socratis* describes spirits, demons, dwelling between the
moon and the earth, who when they wish assume
human form and hold intercourse with women.
It is this narrative of Geoffrey that starts the
whole question as to whether the romance-
writers of the Middle Ages knew the *Metamorphoses* or not. One group of scholars, represented by Kawczynski, think that Geoffrey
used here in this marvellous story not only the
*de deo Socratis* with its theory of demons, but
also the tale of Cupid and Psyche with its
picturesque features. Another group of scholars
whose spokesman is Huet thinks that Geoffrey's
narrative does not need to be explained by re-
course to the Psyche story, in fact his tale does
not resemble the other greatly, for Demetia
speaks of the beauty of her lover so that he was
not an invisible guest as Cupid was.

This whole question as to whether Apuleius'

[ 103 ]

*Metamorphoses* was known in the Middle Ages rages around the study of certain French romances which manifest some clear resemblances to the Psyche story. The chief of these are *Parténopeus de Blois,* the *Chevalier au cygne* and *Huon de Bordeaux.*

In *Parténopeus* the events are much the same as in the Cupid-Psyche story, but the characters are reversed, for it is a lost hero (Parténopeus, nephew of the king of France) who is taken on an enchanted ship to a magical palace, inhabited by invisible beings. At night he is visited by an invisible lady, Melior, Queen of Byzantium. She promises to marry him after some time, but enjoins that meanwhile he shall not see her face. Parténopeus' mother tries to break his devotion by the use of a magical lantern. Parténopeus sees his lady by this and incurs her wrath. Banished from her, he suffers much and is near death, but finally, partly through the aid of Melior's sister, he is re-united to his love. The story closes with a brilliant marriage.

The *Chevalier au cygne* in the original form of the legend recorded the marriage of a king and a fairy, the miraculous birth at one deliverance of six sons and one daughter, the exposure of the children, the persecution of the fairy by

a cruel step-mother, the temporary transformation of the sons into swans and the final vindica-
tion of the mother's truth and honor. In some
versions virtue triumphs through the help of a
Christian hermit.

In *Huon de Bordeaux,* as the *chanson* is told
in the thirteenth century, the hero, Huon, encounters all sorts of adventures on a perilous
journey to Babylon, and undoubtedly would
have perished if he had not been aided by
Oberon, a tiny king of the fairies. With his help
he wins the hand of the daughter of the Emir
of Babylon, returns to France safely, and there
downs his enemies. Oberon is the link with the
Cupid story, for he carries a bow, an ivory
heart hangs from his neck, and he has marvellous powers given him by the fays to know the
hearts of men and their secret thoughts, to
transport himself wherever he wishes, to pos-
sess whatever material objects he desires.
Moreover Oberon claims that he is the son of
Julius Caesar and a fairy! This is to me the
clearest evidence of at least some vague connection in the narrator's mind between his Oberon
and that Cupid with whom Julius Caesar was
proud to claim kinship by Venus and Anchises.

The question of the sources of these and other

old French romances can probably never be settled. One set of interpreters will always see in them such close resemblances to Apuleius' *Metamorphoses* that they will declare the French authors were directly indebted to Apuleius although they never use the names Cupid and Psyche. So Kawczynski. Other scholars will always believe that the common elements in Apuleius and the French romances of the Middle Ages are typical features of folk-lore tales whose origin lies deeply hidden in the life of many people. Such elements are an invisible lover, a taboo against seeing the lover, a magical palace, a cruel step-mother, hard toils, divine or magic aid, final triumph of love. The French scholar Huet in maintaining this point of view argues also that there is no evidence of any knowledge of a manuscript of the *Metamorphoses* in France before the thirteenth century. The catalogues of libraries previous to 1300 do not mention the *Metamorphoses,* although they do list Apuleius' philosophical writings. Richard de Fournival (thirteenth century), who had for his time a remarkable knowledge of classical literature, mentions several works of Apuleius but never the *Metamorphoses*. And in fact it would seem that the first mediaeval mention of

it is in Vincent de Beauvais, in the middle of
the thirteenth century. As we have seen, the
manuscript tradition goes back to an Italian
manuscript of the eleventh century in the
Laurentian Library, which possesses also one
twelfth century copy of this same eleventh
century manuscript. Not until the thirteenth
century do the copies of the *Metamorphoses*
multiply and these copies invariably go back to
the Laurentian. In other words, we have no
definite evidence from reference, library lists,
or manuscript tradition that the *Metamorphoses* was known in France before the thirteenth century. These facts do not preclude a
possible knowledge of the *Metamorphoses,* but
they leave the question of the debt of the French
romances to Apuleius insoluble.

So too the stories that use the motif of a man
transformed into an ass may or may not be indebted to Apuleius' Golden Ass and his Lucius.
In *Le Roman de Tristan* written in the twelfth
century by Beroul of Brittany, Mark has ass's
ears, concealed under a cap. In *Le Roman de
Renart,* Bernard ' l'anne l'archeprete ' is one of
the characters. William of Malmesbury in his
Chronicle of the Kings of England (twelfth
century) relates a story of how two witches

dwelling near Rome changed a lad who was a professional dancer into an ass; how the ass earned money for them by dancing and was finally sold to a rich man, but eventually he became a man again by rolling in water. These mediaeval stories of a man-ass from Saint Augustine down to William of Malmesbury may have a link with Apuleius or they too may have grown out of those tales of transformations into animals which are deeply imbedded in Indo-European folk-lore.

We know that in the Middle Ages stories and festivals of the Ass were popular. For just as in pagan times this beast was regarded as Vesta's darling so in the Christian church the ass, perhaps because of his association with Balaam, his presence in the stable when Christ was born, his bearing the Lord into Jerusalem, had become a revered animal. The Festival of the Ass was indeed celebrated in many towns in France and its ceremonial drawn up for the Church of Sens may still be read in a thirteenth century manuscript. An actual ass was led in procession through the streets, escorted into the church by the clergy, and led to the altar where it stood while " The Prose of the Ass " was chanted:

*Orientibus partibus,*
*Adventavit Asinus,*
*Pulcher et fortissimus*
*Sarcinis aptissimus,*
*Hé, sire Ane, hé!*

*Hic in collibus Sichen,*
*Enutritus sub Ruben,*
*Transiit per Jordanem,*
*Saliit in Bethleem.*
*Hé, sire Ane, hé!*

It undoubtedly did not need the announcement of the priest, "this is the day of gladness; let all be joyful," to encourage the people to join after the Hallelujah in braying in chorus. The account of this festival serves to show us how near to primitive animal folk-lore the mediaeval people were when the church could countenance such a ceremony.

Our knowledge of the influence of Apuleius in the Middle Ages is but slight. Apuleius, the magician, stands out clearly in the literature of the early Middle Ages. His theories of demons and of incubations persist down through the Middle Ages, and library lists and definite references to his philosophical works show that these were known in the eleventh and twelfth centuries. I have not found certain proof of knowledge of the *Metamorphoses,* outside of Italy, between the sixth century and the thirteenth, but the possibility of such knowledge is suggested by the content of the mediaeval French romances. The manuscript tradition of the *Metamorphoses* starts in Italy in the eleventh century, but it is not until the time of Boccaccio and the Renaissance that Apuleius the storyteller is re-born.

# V. APULEIUS THE WRITER
## OF ROMANCE

THE influence of Apuleius in both the Middle Ages and the Renaissance reflects the spirit of each period. To the Middle Ages Apuleius was the magician, working miracles by the aid of the demons whom he invoked. To the Renaissance Apuleius was the entertainer, narrating stories which enthralled and enlivened the imagination.

In the revival of learning during the fifteenth century, when mediaeval tradition, dogma and asceticism were challenged by the spirits of Greece and Rome, a vital feature of the Renaissance was the return of the spirit of joy. Liberty of thought, frank self-expression, delight in beauty, conviviality united in welcoming romance. Naturally the writer of the *Metamorphoses*, once known, made an immediate appeal to a society which wished diversion.

[ 111 ]

It was Poggio who first discovered a manuscript of Apuleius' novel, but Boccaccio is the one who did most in making it known. There is a copy of the *Metamorphoses* written in Boccaccio's own hand and he was soon re-telling Apuleius' stories in Italian to the delight of his readers. The novel gave a wealth of material to the man who, as Symonds says, "was the first who frankly sought to justify the pleasures of the carnal life, whose temperament, unburdened by asceticism, found a congenial element in amorous legends of antiquity." [22] From the time when Poggio and Boccaccio began to make known parts of the *Metamorphoses*, Apuleius exerted three lines of influence throughout the Renaissance and down into the nineteenth century. Short stories were extracted separately from his novel and re-told in various languages. A voluminous literature of the ass developed. And the Cupid and Psyche story inspired manifold forms of literature.

The short story as an independent form or as a part of a loosely woven novel was naturally popular in the Renaissance. The Comic Spirit, *Risus,* enthroned on high dais, pagan, wanton, elegant, was the patron deity of these outbursts of salacious merriment, which tittered over the naughtinesses of human nature or satirized the vices of the clergy. Nothing was too lewd to be told if it was human and humorous. Poggio led the fashion in writing in Latin his *Facetiae*, miniature mirthful tales of the most scandalous but brilliant sort. In two of these (CVI and CVII), which tell how a man made love to a lady who was really a demon, he may be indebted to Apuleius, or he may be using general folk-lore of the Middle Ages.

Boccaccio in the *Decameron*, which appeared about 1352, translated two of Apuleius' stories into Italian. In this novel a group of ten ladies and gentlemen to escape from the horrors of the Plague retires to a villa near Florence and, to enliven their days, exchange stories, each narrating one a day. The story of the lover who revealed himself by sneezing (*Nov.* 10, *giorn.* 5) is taken directly from the *Metamorphoses* (viii. 22–8) and, as in Apuleius, includes the inserted story told by the husband about his neighbor's wife. A more famous story is that of "The lover hid in the cask," which Boccaccio translates almost directly from Apuleius (*Nov.* 2, *giorn.* 7; *Met.*, ix. 4–7). The clever ruse by which the stupid husband is persuaded to go

inside the cask to clean it for a supposed pur-
chaser, while the youthful lover, posing as the
buyer, gains his desire outside is told with
relish. Indeed the episode was considered so
amusing that it was re-told many times. Mor-
lini, a Neapolitan doctor of laws of the sixteenth century, narrated it in Latin in his book
of short stories (*Novella* 35) with a moral at-
tached on the end: " Novella indicat neminem
fraudibus mulierum posse resistere." La Fontaine in the seventeenth century re-wrote it in a
delicious French poem of seventy-four lines,
" Le Cuvier," beginning and ending with the
verse: " Soyez amant, vous serez inventif." And
" Le Cuvier " inspired three comic operas in
France as well as an English " musical entertainment," all in the eighteenth century. The
extremely risqué character of these two stories
in the *Decameron* shows how the Milesian tale
element in the *Metamorphoses* with all its wantonness persisted in favor.

Other types of short stories were also transported from the *Metamorphoses*. Don Quixote's
battle with the wine-skins (Book 4, chapter 8)
is clearly indebted to Lucius' encounter with the
three wine-skins which he mistook for robbers
(*Met.*, II. 32–III. 12). Gil Blas' experiences

in the robbers' cave (Book I, chapters 3–12) take from Apuleius (*Met.*, III. 28–VIII. 15) the cave setting, the old hag cook, the narration of their life histories by three robber chieftains, and the capture of the lady, who tells her own thrilling love-story. Anatole France's "La Rotisserie de la Reine Pédauque" owes something to the fairy lover of the Cupid-Psyche story and more to the incubation motif of *de deo Socratis,* so familiar in the Middle Ages. For M. d'Asterac's adorable Salamanders of the clouds who make such amiable lady-loves for philosophers could be easily recognized as Apuleius' demons even if M. France had not mentioned in his novel his own familiarity with Apuleius' Milesian tales and Apuleius' many examples of the cunning of women, sprinkled like salt in the *Metamorphoses*. These are but a few famous illustrations of the separate episodes extracted from Apuleius and re-told by later writers.

The literature of the ass in Italy owed its inspiration to Apuleius. In 1549 Boiardo translated the Ass of the pseudo-Lucian from Poggio's Latin version and Apuleius' *Metamorphoses,* but this work was virtually forgotten when, shortly after, Firenzuola's translation

of the "Golden Ass" of Apuleius appeared.
Both before and after this popular Italian version, many distinguished writers were using
the ass-motif in transformation stories, in allegory and in satire, or in a combination of all
three treatments.

Before Firenzuola's work was finished in
1525, Macchiavelli was working on a poem in
*terza rima*, called the "Golden Ass," which was
to describe how a Florentine, transformed into
an ass, suffered in his wanderings over the
world, in order to work out his salvation. This
poem, unfinished as it is, shows the transformation motif and the allegorical design. A similar
metamorphosis is depicted in the *opus maca-
ronicum*, a poem in Latin hexameters by Teo-
philus Folenghus, 1521. The hero, Baldo, sees
his friend Boccalo, as a punishment for thieving,
transformed into an ass, rescues him, and
finally by the help of a nymph and a magician
restores him to his own shape. This poem is
something of a parody and something of a satire,
since the poet does not know whether Boccalo,
on changing his hide, also changed his habits.
In this century too appeared the political satire
of Pontano, a dialogue in which Alfonso, duke
of Calabria, is represented as a foolish old man

devoted to an ass which returns his adoration by an ungrateful bite.

Various works in praise of the Ass now begin to appear, an anonymous poem in Italian, one in Latin prose by Enrico Cornelio Agrippa, both exalting the ass and his virtues, recalling his position in Hebrew writings, and exhorting mankind to emulate his strength, his patience, his peaceful nature. These two, serious as they are, are yet the acknowledged precursors of Giordano Bruno's satirical elaborations of the same themes.

Bruno, that free-souled metaphysician who was finally a martyr in the cause of truth, in various writings under his ironical praise of *l'asinità* derides and vituperates superstition, ignorance, sensuality, corruption and all the bondage of society. Two parts of the *Cabala* best show his irony. In the second dialogue, Onorio narrates his Metamorphoses from ass to wandering spirit, then to winged ass, then to man, in short the multiform transmigrations in one of which he was even Aristotle. Through it all he learned that there were no vital differences between men and beasts. In the *Asino cillenico* at the end of the *Cabala,* an ass petitions for admission to the Academy and although the

President and the Academicians portray the difficult entrance requirements and curriculum, the ass is, confident of success because he believes he was once a man, and so with the aid of Mercury he forces his entrance.

In these various writings about the ass, Bruno shows that the ignorance typified by the beast exists in both the Church and the Academy, among the clergy and among the Aristotelians. So to acquire happiness and success, temporal and spiritual, it is necessary to attain *l'asinità* and the greatest asses are the most honored. " Sono esclusi, scherniti e perseguitati coloro che aborrono le volgarità e si mettono per il cammino del vero e nobile sapere. L'asinità è la vera e orribile bestia che sempre vive e sempre trionfa, per sventura degli uomini." [23] It was in his war upon *l'asinità* that Bruno laid down his life.

The Italian literature of the ass takes on many other forms. Carlo Dottori wrote a humorous heroic poem about a war between Padova and Vicenza during which the ass on the standard of Vicenza came to life and by his braying broke off peace negotiations. Salvatore Viale in another poem described a feud between the Borghigiani and Luccianesi which centered in a grotesque contest over the carcass of an ass. Fusconi in an unfinished satire in *terza rima*, called *L'asinaria*, depicted the eternal ass who from the Garden of Eden to the time of Saint George wandered over the earth, experiencing various transformations, now man, now devil, at one time Apollonius of Tyana, always doing evil until Saint George threw him into the well of Saint Patrick. Giambattista Casti wrote two satirical poems on the animal kingdom in which the ass figures as a politician. Ugo Foscolo in his prose work, *Hypercalypsis*, lets the shade of an ass deliver an oration on the folly of men. Guerrazzi describes in Latin the Last Judgment when, after men are judged, Solomon judges the beasts, and the ass as philosopher and orator pleads their cause. All these works seem to have some political application. However remote they are from Apuleius, some of them are perhaps legitimate descendants of his man-ass and its vague symbolism.

However popular Apuleius' short stories and his man-ass plot were from the fourteenth to the eighteenth century, the *Metamorphoses* exerted their greatest influence through the story of Cupid and Psyche. In 1472, Boccaccio in his *Genealogy of the Gods* [24] re-told in Latin, in a simple and delightful way, this tale from Apuleius. Boccaccio acknowledges his debt to the *Metamorphoses,* states that he took the names of Psyche's parents, Apollo and En-delichia, from Martianus Capella, and at the end of his charming narrative adds a long alle-gorical interpretation of his own. From this time on the possibilities of artistic treatment of the story in many different forms and media were seen. Italy, Spain, France, Germany, England in turn appropriated Psyche and gave her new garb. And she supplied inspiration not only to poets and musicians, but to painters and sculp-tors.

Various forms of literary treatment were originated and established in Italy, for there first the story inspired epics, dramas, ballet-operas, poetic letter. The first epic seems to have been written in 1491 by Niccolò da Cor-reggio, a poem called "Psiche." This was fol-lowed by a much more important epic poem in eight books by Ercole Udine, probably first published 1599. The narrative of Apuleius is followed very closely with certain expansions of descriptions like the festival of nymphs and shepherds on Lake Benacus which Venus at-

tends and of the palace where she finds Cupid.
He had been painting portraits of ladies, including one of Leonora di Medici to whom the book
is dedicated. Udine makes a distinct change at
the end, for the child of Cupid and Psyche is
not a daughter but a son, Diletto.

Boccaccio and Udine together inspired Bracciolini to start another epic which he never
finished. Later Marino in his epic *Adone,* published 1623, used the Psyche Märchen. Both
Udine and Marino make Venus wander through
Italy in search of Amor and each poet makes
Venus find her son near his own native birthplace, Udine near Mantua, Marino near Naples.
The episodes of Apuleius' prose narrative were
so easily transferred to heroic poetry that the
epic treatment naturally flourished.

Drama too easily re-cast the Psyche story
into plots. Galeotto dal Carretto wrote the first
Psyche dramas in 1519 producing *Il Tempio di
Amore* which contained a description of Amor's
palace and in 1520 *Le Noze (sic) di Psyche e
di Cupidine,* a comedy. Galeotto simply turned
Apuleius' text into dialogue making no significant additions, only giving somewhat more
prominence to Psyche's parents and to her
sisters' husbands. The father of Psyche is now

not Apollo, but a mortal, Cosmus, her mother, Endilithia.

A hundred years later (1619) Mercadanti published another drama, *Psiche,* which though indebted to Apuleius, Udine and Galeotto, shows a good deal of originality. A definite locality is given to the story; new names are given to the parents and the sisters; the nurse of the princesses has an important part; allegorical figures are introduced; changes in the plot are made; and Psyche's character is developed so that she is more forceful and interesting.

The story was made the basis of musical drama as well as of plays. In 1565 in Florence Alessandro Striggio composed a Ballet-Opera in honor of the marriage of Francesco di Medici and Johanna of Austria. The production is a medley of pantomime, monologues, dialogues, scenic effects, ballet, music and song. Dances of the Hours and Graces, choruses of Amoretti, ballets of allegorical figures, and of satyrs enliven the development of the simple plot. Another musical drama, *La Psiche,* was written by Francesco di Poggio with music by Breni and given at Lucca in 1645. This is more of a drama than Striggio's Interlude.as it has a plot developed in five acts and the ballets are incidental.

New points in the treatment are Zephyr's intercession with Amor, the omission of three tasks, the menace of a real dragon, the transformation of the wicked sisters into cypress trees, the descent of the Olympian gods to earth and their escort of Psyche to heaven. Four years after Poggio's, another musical drama was composed by Diamante Gabrielli for the wedding of Isabella, Archduchess of Austria, and Carlo Secondo, duke of Mantua. It is written very elaborately with five acts and many scenes. Still another cantata of a simpler type, *La Psiche Deificata,* was produced by the Archdeacon Savaro in Bologna 1668. It is divided into two parts, and depends partly on dialogue, partly on pantomime. The outline follows Apuleius' narrative closely, but with considerable shortening.

Another very different form in which the story was re-cast is the poetic letter. Antonio Bruni, undoubtedly getting his idea from Ovid's *Heroides,* wrote an epistle, " Amore à Psiche," based on Apuleius, in which Amor recalls to Psyche their past love-story, predicts the tests which she must undergo and promises his aid.

The various literary forms in which the story

of Cupid and Psyche was used in Italy were adopted and developed in other countries. In Spain epic, drama, musical drama all found favor. As early as the middle of the sixteenth century, Don Juan de Mal Lara wrote a Psyche epic in twelve books, following Apuleius' narrative in all important points. Additions made by Mal Lara are deeds of ancient chivalry and of religious symbolism; long accounts of travels (Psyche's wanderings to the end of the world; the journey of Cupid and Psyche from island to island in the Aegean); the story of a phantom lover of Psyche whom Juno created; and the heroine's purification.

A more distinguished Spanish handling of the material is that of Don Pedro Calderon de la Barca in the seventeenth century. Calderon used the Psyche material three times, first in 1640 in a comedy, twice in an *Auto Sacramental*. The three-act comedy, *Ni Amor se libra de Amor,* is very original in treatment. Calderon omitted all the tasks imposed on Psyche and he developed the human interest by striking additions for the sake of the plot. Two oracles instead of one announce Psyche's fate, with an increase of suspense. Psyche has a mortal lover, Anteus, who is devoted to her and plays an

important rôle. The two suitors of her sisters
fall in love with Psyche, and the two sisters with
Amor. Frissus, the servant of Anteus, and
Psyche's maid, Flora, have a secondary love
affair. Psyche is exposed on a lonely island.
Amor to console Psyche first lets her see a
mirage of her old home and family and then
conveys her parents, sisters, brothers-in-law and
Anteus on a boat to the island. Anteus tells
Psyche she is wedded to a monster and so persuades her to try to see her lover. The narrative
then follows Apuleius but the ending is happy
and rapid, for Amor after vanishing with his
palace returns, and blesses all, even promising
Anteus a princess for a bride!

As original as his drama, are the two *Autos*
of Calderon. Both have the same object, the
glorification of the Eucharist, and the same development of action. Both omit the oracle. In
the first, written in Madrid, the King is the
World, his three daughters are the three Ages.
The oldest, the time of nature's rule, is wed
to Paganism; the second to Judaism; the
third, Psyche, is unwed. Her marriage, which is
the dénouement, has a double significance: the
marriage of the Church to Christ and of the
Individual Soul to God. A demon, Hate, leads

Psyche into the sin of doubt and for a time separates her from her bridegroom.

In the second *Auto* written for Toledo, the father is the World. The two older daughters, Idolatry and the Synagogue, are wed to *La Gentilidad* and *El Judaismo*. Psyche, or *La Fè*, is the Will. *La Apostasia* and *El Odio* work against Amor to prevent his founding the Church and wedding the Soul. Both *Autos* appear to have been written in a reverent spirit of Catholicism.

Another very original and elaborate Spanish use of the tale is a comedy by Antonio de Solis, 1659, *Triunfos de Amor, y Fortuna*. De Solis, who acknowledges Ovid and Apuleius as his sources, interweaves the stories of Endymion and Psyche and makes the whole a struggle between Amor and Fortuna. The plot, which is too elaborate to condense briefly, owed much to Calderon, but showed also much originality.

In France, the ballet-opera reached its most magnificent development, and a new literary treatment appeared in the form of a romance. In 1656 Benserade produced a Ballet Royal in two parts, one showing Amor's palace, the other depicting Amor, who endeavours to amuse Psyche by the representation of many marvel-

lous exploits of his own. By far the most splendid production of the Psyche story is the drama
planned and written by Molière with the words
of the songs by Quinault and the music by
Lulli. This play was produced in 1671 before
Louis XIV in the Tuileries and in the Palais
Royal. No brief account can tell the intricacies
of the five acts or the splendor of the interludes
and ballets. One feature of the plot is that the
two princes, Cleomene and Agenor, whom the
older sisters try to secure, fall in love with
Psyche, and attempt to defend her from her
fate and therefore meet their death at Amor's
hands. There are rustic dances of dryads,
sylvans, river-gods and naiads; a grotesque
dance of six cyclopes and four fairies; a ballet
of four Loves and four Zephyrs; a dance of
Furies in the lower world and finally a grand
ballet, preceded by songs of the Olympians and
the Muses, and completed by dances of Mae-
nads and Egyptians, of Punchinelli, of Mars
and his warriors. While Molière owes something
to his predecessors, only Calderon approaches
him in originality and beauty of treatment.

*Psyché, Tragédie lyrique,* was produced in
1678. It was first ascribed to Corneille, then
claimed by Fontenelle. The music is by Lulli.

The whole is much indebted to Molière, in fact seems like a simplification of Molière's great work.

La Fontaine who, as we have seen, re-wrote one of Apuleius' short stories in his poem " Le Cuvier," in 1669 published a romance called *Les Amours de Psyché et Cupidon.* If La Fontaine took from Apuleius himself the idea of treatment in the. form of a novel, he nevertheless was original in the handling, for his story is told rapidly in only two books, new and delightful episodes are introduced, and the form varies between prose and poetry. The setting is simple. Four friends are accustomed to meet for literary discussions. One of them, Polyphile, asks permission to read to the others a new work of his own on the Adventures of Psyche. The reading is interrupted by discussion and comment. La Fontaine in his delightful preface summarizes well his purpose and his plan: " Mon principal but est toujours de plaire: pour en venir là, je considère le goût du siècle. . . . Venons aux inventions. Presque toutes sont d'Apulée, j'entends les principales et les meilleures. Il y a quelques épisodes de moi, comme l'aventure de la grotte, le vieillard et les deux bergères, le temple de Vénus et son origine,

la description des enfers, et tout ce qui arrive
à Psyché pendant le voyage qu'elle y fait, et à
son retour jusqu'à la conclusion de l'ouvrage.
La manière de conter est aussi de moi, et les
circonstances, et ce que disent les person-
nages. . . . J'ai tâché seulement de faire en
sorte qu'il plût, et que même on y trouvât du
solide aussi bien que de l'agréable. C'est pour
cela que j'y ai enchâssé des vers en beaucoup
d'endroits, et quelques autres enrichisse-
ments, comme le voyage des quatre amis,
leur dialogue touchant la compassion et le rire,
la description des enfers, celle d'une partie de
Versailles."

The impression one gains from reading the
whole is of much beauty, of amused satire on
womankind, and of delicate irony playing over
Psyche's curiosity, innocent vanity and femi-
nine charm. A grotesque change in the plot is
that when Psyche opens Proserpina's box of
beauty, fumes envelop her which dye her skin
black, and she suffers this horrible blight until
finally Jupiter restores her fairness and allows
her to wed Love.

The use of the Psyche story in German literature takes us down through the nineteenth century, for before that time there was only one

notable attempt to use the tale and that was never consummated. Wieland, fascinated in his youth by the Märchen, conceived the idea of treating it allegorically in a great narrative poem about the history of the Soul. This work, which he began in 1767, was never finished. Parts were worked over in later poems, and the fragments are printed in Gruber's edition of his collected works. From all these Wieland's conception is seen: the story was told by the younger Aspasia, priestess of Diana at Ecbatana, and the scene was laid in the Golden Age. Psyche is a fairy and Amor's love for her is Platonic, since the whole is an allegory of the human Soul and divine Love.

A pupil and admirer of Wieland decided to undertake the work which his master never finished. Ernst Schulze at the age of eighteen when a student at Göttingen (1807) wrote his *Psyche,* "Ein griechisches Märchen in sieben Büchern." It is a work of precocious genius with amusing innovations. Psycharion (a new name for the heroine) grows up in the Vale of Tempe among shepherds until Love once beholds her at her bath, falls in love, transports her to his palace and makes her his own. The oracle is omitted and also the baleful influence of the sisters. Psyche once happens on a grotto wherein stands a frightful marble statue holding a gleaming crystal in which changing scenes appear. In one of these, Psyche beholds herself on a bed beside a horrible dragon. The statue is the Goddess Scepticism and under her influence Psyche now attempts to see her husband. Another new feature is Psyche's first task, which is to take a withered garland from Venus' temple, make it bloom again and offer it to Scepticism. This is done by Ceres' aid. After other tasks and much suffering, Psyche is transported to the Garden of Venus, where Aglaia presents herself as her mother and tells her Apollo is her father. Venus is reconciled. Amor carries her to Olympus, her future home.

In 1851 Dr. Johann Christian Elster published an epic poem in five books written first in Latin hexameters, then translated into German hexameters. Elster emphasizes the ethical significance which he found in the story and to do this adds long, rhetorical speeches. For example, Venus, no longer the cruel step-mother, pronounces a long discourse to Psyche in which she shows by allusions to Phaëthon and Niobe that ambition brings danger, and by the story of Hercules that death must be conquered by courage. The delicacy and humor of Apuleius' narrative are lost.

A recent epic rendering is Robert Hamerling's *Amor und Psyche,* 1882, written in seven books in unrhymed trochaic lines of five feet. The material is treated very freely and allegorically. The meetings of Psyche and Persephone and of Amor and Jupiter are much expanded. Hamerling gives Psyche butterfly wings which grow after she is united to Love. The naïveté of the Märchen is lost in the mysticism of the philosopher. Love, the first time he sees Psyche, says: " All' ihr Wesen, all' ihr Tun ist Seele." When Psyche asks her lover who he is, he answers:

*" Wer ich bin? " entgegnet drauf der Liebste;*
*" Ich bin du — und du bist ich, mein Seelchen! "*

A curious and fanciful treatment is that of Hans Georg Meyer, 1899. The poem is in conventional epic form, five books of hexameters, but the unique feature is the German setting given to the first scenes and the Horatian method of plunging *in medias res* at the very beginning. Psyche in her task of seeking the

golden wool of the rams of Helios comes to a
German district near the North Sea. Half dead
from her wanderings, she is taken into the hut
of a fisherman who lives with his aged mother
and two children. The shade of the fisherman's
dead wife, Bertha, had previously appeared to
direct Psyche on her way. Psyche tells her past
history to the old mother. The Germans have no
difficulty in understanding Psyche's language
and finally Beda is persuaded to take Psyche on
his boat to the island whither Bertha had directed her. After this the Germans disappear
from the story, except that when Psyche goes
to the Lower World in pursuit of Proserpina's
beauty, she encounters Bertha and gives her
happy news of her family.

The ending of Meyer's epic is no less startling
than the beginning. It is Jupiter, not Venus who
sends Psyche to Hades and to become immortal
she must drink a draught of the Styx. Just as
she is about to quaff this cup, persuaded by
Proserpina, Eros appears and prevents her
from drinking. He does not wish her to become
a goddess with the knowledge of misery which
divinity brings. This is a pessimistic note, new
in the story. The future of Cupid and Psyche is

left vague, the poem ending on this note of un-
happiness and despair.

All these German renderings in epic form
have originality, but they have lost the fresh-
ness, the lightness, the brilliancy of Apuleius'
story.

## VI. THE MOST PLEASAUNT AND DELECTABLE TALE OF THE MARRIAGE OF CUPIDE AND PSYCHES

### Done in English

THIS transcript from the title page of William Adlington's translation of the Psyche episode may well head the account of the uses of the story in English literature, for the best of the English renderings, from Spenser to Keats, have caught the charm of the tale. William Adlington himself in his 1566 translation of the *Metamorphoses* still conveys to English readers more fully than does any other prose version the winsome gladness of the fairy-story. There is a delicious mingling of piety and humor in his prefatory letter to the reader. He intends " to utter and open the meaning " of " so sportfull a jest " " to the simple and ignorant, whereby they may not take the same, as a thing only to jest and laugh at — but by the pleasantness thereof bee rather induced to the knowledge of their present estate, and thereby transform themselves into the right and perfect shape of men." But while Adlington declares that "this book of Lucius is a figure of man's life," he never loses his joy in " sportfull jests " and " franke and flourishing stile." His vigorous humor, virility of feeling and richness of phraseology make his translation, quaint as its diction seems now, entertaining reading, whether or no it is as regenerating as the author hoped. Pursuing delight instead of shunning her, he easily disavowed all claims to literalness. " I have not so exactly passed through the Author, as to point every sentence according as it is in Latine, or so absolutely translated every word as it lieth in the prose, considering the same in our vulgar tongue would have appeared very obscure and darke, and thereby consequently loathsome to the Reader, but nothing erring as I trust from the true and naturall meaning of the Author, have used more common and familiar words, yet not so much as I might doe, for the plainer setting forth of the same."

Something of Adlington's quality may be seen from the beginning of the story.

" There was sometimes, a certaine Kinge, inhabityng in the West partes, who had to wife

THE MARRIAGE OF CUPID AND PSYCHE
By Raphael in the VILLA FARNESINA

a noble Dame, by whome he had three daughters
exceedinge fayre: Of whome the two elder
weare of such comely shape and beautie, as
they did excell and passe all other women living,
whereby they weare thought, worthely, to de-
serve the praise and commendation of every
person, and deservedly to be preferred above
the residew of the common sorte: Yet the singu-
lar passinge beautie and maidenly Majestie of
the yongest daughter, did so far surmounte and
excell them two, as no eerthly creature coulde
by any meanes sufficiently expresse or set out
the same, by reason whereof (after the fame of
this excellent maiden was spred abrode in every
part of the Citie,) the Citizens and Strangers
there, beinge inwardly pricked by zelous af-
fection to beholde her famous person, came
daily by thousandes, hundreds and scores, to
her fathers Pallaice, who as astonied with admiration of her incomparable beautie did no
lesse worshippe and reverence her, with crosses,
signes and tokens, and other divine adorations,
accordinge to the custome of the olde used rites
and ceremonies, then if she weare Ladie Venus
indeede: And shortly after the fame was
spredde into the next Cities and borderinge
Regions, that the Goddesse whome the deepe

seas had borne and brought foorth, and the frothe of the spurginge waves had nourished, to the intent to showe her highe Magnificencie and divine power in earth, to suche as earst did honour and woorshippe her: was now conversant amongst mortall men, or else that the earth and not the seas, by a newe concurse and influence of the celestiall Planetes, had budded and yelded foorth a newe Venus, endewed with the flower of virginitie."

After Adlington had introduced Apuleius to England, the Psyche story received the same varied forms of treatment that it had on the continent. It was rendered in drama (tragedy and comedy), in epic (heroic and pious), in poetic tale and in prose story. Also it inspired rapt lyric.

Although Edmund Spenser did not make any long use of the story, he showed its appeal to himself by the charm of his allusions. In *Muiopotmos*, he speaks of Venus' "jealous feare" about Cupid, for she was

> Not yet unmindfull how not long agoe
> Her sonne to Psyche secrete love did beare,
> And long it close conceal'd, till mickle woe
> Thereof arose, and manie a rufull teare.

In *The Faerie Queene*,[25] 1590, he briefly tells the whole story and makes Venus so completely reconciled to her daughter-in-law that she entrusts a pet fosterling to Psyche for proper education!

*And his true love, faire Psyche, with him playes,*
*Fayre Psyche to him lately reconcyled,*
*After long troubles and unmeet upbrayes,*
*With which his mother Venus her revyld,*
*And eke himself her cruelly exyld:*
*But now in stedfast love and happy state*
*She with him lives, and hath him borne a chyld,*
*Pleasure, that doth both gods and men aggrate,*
*Pleasure, the daughter of Cupid and Psyche late.*
*Hether great Venus brought this infant fayre,*
*The yonger daughter of Chrysogonee,*
*And unto Psyche with great trust and care*
*Committed her, yfostered to bee,*
*And trained up in trew feminitee:*
*Who no less carefully her tendered*
*Then her owne daughter Pleasure, to whom shee*
*Made her companion, and her lessoned*
*In all the lore of love and goodly womanhead.*

Spenser's exquisite lines were to inspire later two second-rate narrative poems in the Spenserian stanza. But long before those were written, Apuleius began to appear upon the English stage. It is a temptation to try to find in *A Midsummer-Night's Dream* some sure reminiscence of the *Metamorphoses* of Apuleius, for the fairy-tale atmosphere is here; Oberon may perhaps come from "Huon de Bordeaux" and so have the vague association with Cupid which Huon's Oberon had; and Bottom "translated" with an ass-head of his own dimly recalls lover Lucius changed to ass. But I can find no evidence of direct debt to Apuleius on Shakspeare's part. A famous and brilliant dramatic rendering of the Cupid and Psyche story came out in England in 1636. This was Thomas Heywood's *Loves Mistris, or the Queens Masque*. The Masque was at once so successful that it was presented before James First and his queen three times in eight days and for the second production the Master Surveyor of the King's work, " that admirable Artist, Mr. Inego Jones," says Heywood, staged the play. "Who to every Act, nay almost to every Sceane, by his excellent Inventions, gave such an extraordinary Luster; upon every occasion changing the stage, to the admiration of all the Spectators; that, as I must ingeniously confesse, It was above my apprehension to conceive, so to their sacred Majesties, and the rest of the Auditory." In this prefatory letter to the " generous Reader," Heywood acknowledges his source and states his purpose. " The Argument is taken from Apuleius, an excellent Morrall, if truely understood, and may be called a Golden Truth, contened in a leaden fable, which though it bee not altogether conspicuous to the vulgar, yet to those of learning and judgment, no lesse apprehended in the Paraphrase, then approved in the Originall."

The " golden truth " is made very clear in the masque, for Apuleius himself ("with a paire of Asse eares in his hand ") re-transformed to wisdom, a defender of poetry and the Muses, and Midas, a " dull covetous foole," the type of complete ignorance, act as a sort of chorus to the play and keep up "a running comment of criticism and exposition " as Symonds says. Apuleius himself announces this purpose of their presence at the end of the first scene:

*Wee too contend; Art heere, there Ignorance:*
*Bee you the Judges, wee invite you all*
*Unto this banquet accademicall.*

The play proper begins with a scene in which Admetus, Psyche's father, Astioche and Petrea,

her sisters, Menetius and Zelotis, her sisters'
husbands, receive the oracle of Apollo at
Delphi (not Miletus). And after this the plot
follows the general outline of Apuleius' tale.
But the development is interrupted by dances
introduced to appease the bored Midas and by
long moral explanations of the meaning, given
by Apuleius for Midas' benefit. So when at the
end of the charming fairy scene in Cupid's
palace, Midas protests:

*Ile hang my selfe, ere Ile see out thy Play,*

Apuleius to detain him introduces a dance of
asses, — a Proud Asse, a Prodigall Asse, a
Drunken Asse, an Ignorant Asse, all with a clear
moral. Yet Midas needs more instruction, for he
sees little in the story:

*Thou brings't heere on the stage*
*A young greene-sicknesse baggage to run after*
*A little ape-fac'd boy thou tearm'st a god;*
*Is not this most absurd?*

And it is necessary for Apuleius to explain the
great allegory:

*Mis-understanding foole, thus much conceive,*
*Psiche is Anima, Psiche is the Soule,*

*The Soule a Virgin, longs to be a bride,*
*The soule's Immortall, whom then can shee woo*
*But Heaven? Whom wed, but Immortality:*
*Oh blame not Psiche then, if mad with rage,*
*Shee long for this so divine marriage.*

Midas thereafter is alternately entertained by
the spectacular and enlightened as to the " excellent morrall." There are dances of " Pan,
Clowne, Swaines, and Country-wenches," of
" Love's Contrarieties," namely a King and a
beggar, a young man and an old woman, a lean
man and a fat woman, a dance of Vulcan and
his Cyclopes, and finally of Cupid, Psyche, the
gods and goddesses. Midas, who had begged for
" some quaint device, some kick-shaw or other
to keepe me waking," must have been mollified
by all this pageantry as well as by the Clown
who steals the box of beauty for his Amaryllis
and is deceived by a counterfeit box " full of
ugly painting " with which he unconsciously
disfigures himself.

After the action is over, a brief epilogue is
necessary, a dialogue between Midas and Apuleius who are still at variance over the worth of
the play. Cupid acts as judge, pronouncing
sentence:

*Keepe thou the Asses eares, the Lawrell, thou,*

and then tells the audience that if they commend this his doome, as spring comes on,

*Each shall enjoy his best lov'd Valentine.*

The play is good reading with its original combination of Apuleius' ass-motif and fairytale, its extravaganzas, its magic and its tomfoolery. With the pageantry suggested by the dances it must easily have enchanted the English court.

A year after *Loves Mistris* was printed, appeared " an Epic Poem of Cupid and his Mistress written by Shakerley Marmion." Marmion was a close friend of Heywood, for in the 1637 edition is included among other " commendatory verses " a poem signed Thomas Heywood which runs:

*Love and the soul are two things, both divine,*
*And now thy task, dear friend, which once was mine.*
*What I writ was dramatical; thy Muse*
*Was in an epic strain, which they still use,*
*Who write heroic poems. Thine is such,*
*Which when I read, I could not praise too much.*

Heywood goes on to laud Marmion's high Argument and the "sublime and weighty rapture" of his subject, but his friend as a matter of fact gave but little space to the Moral. Marmion simply sets forth at the beginning "the Explanation of the Argument" in a long paragraph of allegory.

"By the City is meant the World; by the King and Queen, God and Nature; by the two elder Sisters, the Flesh and the Will; by the last, the Soul which is the most beautiful," and so on.

The way thus cleared, Marmion begins his charming epic of two books in the heroic couplet. He follows Apuleius closely except for a wealth of added mythological allusions and of purple patches of description such as Cupid's quiver, the palace of Proserpina, Venus' toilet, and for certain naïve moral comments of his own:

*Promises are frail,*
*And virtue flies when love once blows the sail.*

*Passions are infus'd*
*According to the stories we are us'd*
*To read, and many men do amorous prove,*
*By viewing acts, and monuments of love.*

> All (*though to their cost*)
> *Desire forbidden things, but women most.*

To show all the Metamorphoses which
Psyche has undergone, mention must be made
of a pious piece which was another production
of the seventeenth century. This was *Psyche,
or Love's Mystery,* "in XXIV Cantos: Displaying the Intercourse betwixt Christ and the
Soul." Dr. Joseph Beaumont, in his introduction, stated his Christian purpose: " I endeavor
to represent a Soul led by divine Grace and her
guardian Angel (in fervent Devotion) through
the difficult temptations and assaults of Lust,
of Pride, of Heresy, of Persecution, and of
Spiritual Dereliction, to a holy and happy De-
parture from temporal Life, to heavenly Felicity: Displaying by the way, the Magnalia
Christi, his Incarnation and Nativity, his Flight
into Egypt, his Fasting and Temptation, his
chief Miracles, his being Sold and Betrayed, his
Institution of the Holy Eucharist, his Passion,
his Resurrection and Ascension; which were his
mighty Testimonies of his Love to the Soul."
The poem was revised for a second edition by
the poet's son, Charles, who has as devout a
purpose and more priggishness. He says in a

foreword: " The whole design of the Poem is to recommend the Practice of Piety and Morality by describing the most remarkable Passages of our Saviors Life, and by painting particular Virtues and Vices in their proper colours: a Design which I could wish all Writers of English verse would propound to themselves; for 'tis undoubtedly true, that no Wit or Fancy whatsoever can make atonement for those obscene, prophane and scurrillous expressions which are too visible in some late English poems."

These two prefaces give the character of the poem.

Another seventeenth century production is notorious for the derisive satire which it aroused. This is Thomas Shadwell's *Psyche, a Tragedy,* a work " imitated from the French of Molière," and finished, as Shadwell assures us, in the space of five weeks. The unfortunate drama was soon burlesqued in Thomas Duffet's *Psyche Debauch'd, a Comedy* (1678), " a mass of low scurrility and abuse," and was derided by John Dryden in his poem, " Mac Flecknoe, or a Satire upon the True Blue Protestant Poet, T. S." Sir Walter Scott in his notes on Dryden says that Shadwell "having no talents for poetry, and no ear for versification, 'Psyche' is

one of the most contemptible of the frivolous
dramatic class to which it belongs." The lines
which Sir Walter quotes are sufficient proof that
Dryden had reason for describing Shadwell as
" Mature in dulness from his tender years " and
the " last great prophet of tautology."

NICANDER: *Madam, I to this solitude am come,*
*Humbly from you to hear my latest*
*doom.*

PSYCHE: *The first command which I did give,*
*Was, that you should not see me here;*
*The next command you will receive,*
*Much harsher will to you appear.*

NICANDER: *How long, fair Psyche, shall I sigh in*
*vain?*
*How long of scorn and cruelty com-*
*plain?*
*Your eyes enough have wounded me,*
*You need not add your cruelty.*
*You against me too many weapons*
*choose,*
*Who am defenseless against each you*
*use.*

It seems no wonder that Swinburne dubbed
it " a lyrical drama . . . than which nothing

more portentous in platitude ever crawled into print."

I have spoken of two poems on the Psyche Märchen written in the Spenserian stanza. The first was Glocester Ridley's, 1747. Ridley acknowledged his debt to Spenser and shows the latter's influence in his archaic diction and details as well as in the meter of his fifty-one stanzas. The poem is allegorical. In 1805, Mrs. Henry Tighe brought out a much more pretentious effort in Spenserian stanza, " Psyche or the Legend of Love, a Poem in Six Cantos." Through two cantos, Mrs. Tighe follows closely Apuleius' narrative, but after that the poem becomes a cross between a mediaeval tale of chivalry and a female Pilgrim's Progress. A stranger knight with his squire, Constance, now devotes himself to Psyche's service, defends her from the power of Passion in the form of a ravening lion, from Ambition and from Slander, delivers her out of the dark cave of Jealousy, rescues her from the island of Indifference, and finally before the temple of Venus reveals himself as her faithful knight and lover.

Mrs. Tighe has decided facility of rhythm, little taste, considerable morality and overmuch sentimentality. Perhaps this is too severe judgment, for her days are not our days. But two stanzas from different cantos may themselves illustrate her style:

*Her suit obtained, in full contentment blest,*
*Her eyes at length in placid slumbers close.*
*Sleep, hapless fair! sleep on thy lover's breast;*
*Ah, not again to taste such pure repose!*
*Till thy sad heart by long experience knows*
*How much they err, who, to their interest blind,*
*Slight the calm peace which from retirement flows!*
*And while they think their fleeting joys to bind,*
*Banish the tranquil bliss which heaven for man*
　　　*designed.*

*With meek submissive woe she heard her doom,*
*Nor to the holy minister replied;*
*But in the myrtle grove's mysterious gloom*
*She silently retired her grief to hide.*
*Hopeless to tread the waste without a guide,*
*All unrefreshed and faint from toil she lies:*
*When lo! her present wants are all supplied,*
*Sent by the hand of Love a turtle flies*
*And sets delirious food before her wondering eyes.*

Even although the "turtle" is a dove, the prosaic diction of these lines, which are a little worse than Mrs. Tighe's best, is damning, and the poem deserves only the faint praise of fatal facility and sustained effort.

Psyche, by the beginning of the nineteenth century, was so familiar a vision that she was seen and sung by poetasters and poets. Within twenty years the jingles of Hudson Gurney, 1799, were perpetrated and the Ode of Keats was composed. Gurney had the virtue of seeing the folk element in the tale so that he tried a ballad form. The narrative parts are all in strophes of four lines with alternate rhymes. He had not however the genius to turn Apuleius' exotic style back to the simplicity of ballad song. Great moments are basely transcribed. Witness these:

*Thus speaks the Invisible and sighs,*
  *And clasps her in his warm embrace*
*While the large tear-drops from his eyes*
  *Fall frequent on her burning face.*

*But on the Sovereign of the skies*
  *What fleshly optics dare to gaze?*
*And Psyche with averted eyes*
  *Shrinks trembling from th' excessive blaze.*

Mrs. Tighe shines by comparison with such tastelessness as this. Even the consummation of Love's union with Psyche is as uninspired:

[ 151 ]

*In frantic passion's giddy whirl*
  *Past, quickly past, his transient stay,*
*He still eludes the curious girl,*
  *And steals unseen, unfelt, away.*

It seems almost incredible to us after shuddering at these lines that the same story was the inspiration of John Keats as he "stood tiptoe upon a little hill" and felt

> *Uplifted from the world,*
> *Walking upon the white clouds wreath'd and curl'd.*

To his rapt mood came the thought of Apuleius' exaltation in the tale.

*So felt he, who first told, how Psyche went*
*On the smooth wind to realms of wonderment;*
*What Psyche felt, and Love, when their full lips*
*First touch'd; what amorous and fondling nips*
*They gave each other's cheeks; with all their sighs,*
*And how they kist each other's tremulous eyes:*
*The silver lamp, — the ravishment, — the wonder,*
*The darkness, — loneliness, — the fearful thunder:*
*Their woes gone by, and both to heaven upflown,*
*To bow for gratitude before Jove's throne.*

There is the pure lyric treatment of the theme — simple, sensuous, passionate. Even

when Keats, in writing drama, thought of
Psyche, he conveyed his sense of excitement.
In *Otho the Great* Rudolph says:

> Methought I heard
> As I came in, some whispers — what of that?
> 'Tis natural men should whisper; at the kiss
> Of Psyche given by Love, there was a buzz
> Among the gods!

Then there is the *Ode*. When ecstasy's utmost
we clutch at the core, criticism is awed to
silence. Psyche received no more profound
adoration from her ardent worshippers in the
old story than Keats offers here. The reverent
spirit in which he approached his theme was
recorded by himself in a letter of April 30,
1819:

" The following poem, the last I have written,
is the first and only one with which I have taken
even moderate pains; I have, for the most part,
dashed off my lines in a hurry; this one I have
done leisurely; I think it reads the more richly
for it, and it will I hope encourage me to write
other things in even a more peaceable and
healthy spirit. You must recollect that Psyche
was not embodied as a goddess before the time
of Apuleius the Platonist, who lived after the

Augustan Age, and consequently the goddess was never worshipped or sacrificed to with any of the ancient fervour, and perhaps never thought of in the old religion: I am more orthodox than to let a heathen goddess be so neglected."

In an ode of sixty-seven lines, Keats has embodied the ineffable tenderness of young love between two young and winged gods and a new symbolism of a poet's worship for unworshipped Psyche:

*Yes, I will be thy priest, and build a fane*
  *In some untrodden region of my mind,*
*Where branched thoughts, new grown with pleasant*
    *pain,*
  *Instead of pines shall murmur in the wind:*
*Far, far around shall those dark-clustered trees*
  *Fledge the wild-ridged mountains steep by steep*
*And there by zephyrs, streams, and birds, and*
    *bees,*
  *The moss-lain Dryads shall be lull'd to sleep;*
*And in the midst of this wide quietness*
  *A rosy sanctuary will I dress*
*With the wreath'd trellis of a working brain,*
  *With buds, and bells, and stars without a name,*
*With all the gardener Fancy e'er could feign,*
  *Who breeding flowers, will never breed the same:*

[ 154 ]

*And there shall be for thee all soft delight*
  *That shadowy thought can win,*
*A bright torch, and a casement ope at night,*
  *To let the warm Love in!*

No other poet has approached Keats' lyric
melody for Psyche. Mrs. Browning in her verse
translations of various passages of Apuleius
shows delicate sensitiveness and achieves beautiful lines, but her poems are but fragments.
The later English versions are narratives of
varied forms and appeals: three poetic renderings by William Morris, Sir Lewis Morris and
Robert Bridges and Walter Pater's prose story.

William Morris in his *Earthly Paradise*,
figuring as " The idle singer of an empty day "
and denying all moral purpose for his rhymed
couplets ("Why should I strive to set the
crooked straight? "), puts the story of Cupid
and Psyche in the mouth of one of his old men.
It is May-Day when perchance

              *The Lord of Love went by*
*To take possession of his flowery throne,*
*Ringed round with maids, and youths, and min-*
      *strelsy;*

and the old man, turning from his window's
view of youths and maids, flower-crowned,
caroling, says:

*Too fair a tale the lovely time doth ask*
*For this of mine to be an easy task,*
*Yet in what words soever this is writ,*
*As for the matter, I dare say of it*
*That it is lovely as the lovely May.*

The changes which Morris makes in Apuleius' narrative are not in plot or tone, but in expansion of the pictorial effects. His instinct for decorative art made him see in Apuleius' story the same possibilities that had prompted Raphael and del Vaga to use it for mural decoration. So Morris paints picture after picture expanded from hint or line: nature setting for Cupid's first view of Psyche,

*amidst a fair green close*
*Hedged round about with woodbine and red rose;*

for the dawn of Psyche's first day at Cupid's palace; and for her wanderings through the yellow cornfields; descriptions of gorgeous objects: gifts offered to Apollo, Cupid's palace, the royal bed in it; and pictures of persons, to wit the one of Venus.

Morris finds himself unable to describe the " joy unspeakable " which Psyche experienced when

[ 156 ]

> *on her trembling lips she felt the kiss*
> *Of very Love, and mortal yet, for bliss*
> *Must fall a-weeping.*

Instead, he develops a mystic wistfulness in Psyche in heaven even when she " stood at last a very goddess there " in " that sweet new-born immortality."

*And unknown feelings seized her, and there came*
*Sudden remembrance, vivid as a flame,*
*Of everything that she had done on earth,*
*Although it all seemed changed in weight and worth,*
*Small things becoming great, and great things small;*
*And godlike pity touched her therewithal*
*For her old self, for sons of men that die.*

Such musing is the final effect of the tale on the men who were listening:

*And in those old hearts did the story move*
*Remembrance of the mighty deeds of love,*
*And with these thoughts did hopes of life arise,*
*Till tears unseen were in their ancient eyes,*
*And in their yearning hearts unspoken prayers,*
*And idle seemed the world with all its cares.*

The atmosphere of the whole story is, however, rather that of the merry month of May, and the impression produced is that of a series of beautiful pictures, painted in long frieze or wrought in tapestry.

The story in *The Earthly Paradise* seems to me the best of the English narratives in poetry. Lewis Morris, Welshman, Oxford scholar, lawyer, knight, in his *Epic of Hades*, 1877, wrote in iambic pentameters a modern allegory of Tennysonian tinge. His eyes

> H*ad seen the soul of man, the deathless soul,*
> D*efeated, struggling, purified, and blest*

and his Psyche is more saint than fay.

Robert Bridges in 1886 published his *Eros and Psyche*, a long narrative on a rather monotonous level. The arrangement by quarters of the year and by months seems artificial, and prosaic additions such as an acrostic and "a portrait of the phenomena which followed the great eruption of Krakatoa" are blemishes. The most fundamental change from Apuleius is the one announced by the poet himself: "In the way of ethic I have made a gentler characterization of Psyche, who deserves more care in handling the motives of her conduct than was perhaps felt in Apuleius' time and country." Bridges makes intense purity the keynote of her character and philosophical reflection the habit

of her mind. The ending of the poem is typical
of his moral musings and quiet charm.

*So now in steadfast love and happy state*
*They hold for aye their mansion in the sky,*
*And send down heavenly peace on those who mate,*
*In virgin love, to find their joy thereby:*
*Whom gently Eros shooteth, and apart*
*Keepeth for them from all his sheaf that dart*
*Which Psyche in his chamber pickt to try.*

A word about prose translations in English.
Adlington has been made accessible and readable by Gaselee's revision of " The Golden Ass."
In 1903, Charles Stuttaford published a graceful prose translation of the story of Cupid and
Psyche in a volume elegant in printing and illustration. In 1909–1910 Mr. H. E. Butler
brought out translations of the *Apologia*, *Florida* and *Metamorphoses* which from their careful scholarship and readable English are the
standard modern translations of Apuleius.

For a prose version in a literary setting we
turn back to Walter Pater's version in his novel
*Marius the Epicurean* (1885). There the Cupid
and Psyche story is read by two Roman lads,
poring happily over their " golden book " as
they lounged together in an old granary. And

young Marius, as we have seen, was later in the story to meet Apuleius himself and talk with his literary idol.

A cunning stylist, with the artist's love of careful workmanship, Pater must first have been attracted to the "curious felicity" and "jeweller's work" of Apuleius' words. I find in him the finest critique of Apuleius' style. It was natural too that one to whom, as to the Greeks, visible beauty seemed to harbor much of divinity, should find in the Cupid and Psyche story a loveliness of vision that compelled a re-casting of the tale for others. It is true romance for Pater as for Marius in his story — "the ideal of a perfect imaginative love, centered upon a beauty entirely flawless and clean"; and the "lovely visible imagery" which he saw and the "gentle idealism" which he felt made him translate into delicate and exquisite English, often more simple than Apuleius' elaborations, "the floating star-matter" of the tale.

# VII. THE STORY OF CUPID AND PSYCHE IN ART

## 1. IN ANCIENT ART

CUPID and Psyche are very familiar figures in ancient art, but, strange to say, there seems to be no certain illustration of Apuleius' story about them before the time of the Renaissance. For the moment, therefore, we must lay aside all remembrance of the episodes of the Märchen as Apuleius re-told it and go back from Rome to Greece, from the second century after Christ to the fourth century before Christ, from Apuleius to Plato, to see what the words Eros and Psyche connoted in ancient thought and art.

The personification of the two Greek words Ἔρως and Ψυχή, Love and the Soul, was established by Plato. In the *Phaedrus,* that delightful dialogue where, by the Ilissus under the plane tree, amid the shrill summer music of the cicadas, Socrates ever so ironically and tactfully teaches young Phaedrus something of

what love and the soul are, the great teacher
depicts the Soul with wings, suggests that Love
makes these wings grow and pictures the happiness of Psyche, the Soul, swayed by Love.
This is delicate, mystical symbolism.

The relation of Eros and Psyche becomes
more definite and personal in the Greek epigrams of the second and first century before
Christ. In these exquisite little poems Psyche
is represented as tortured, or as suffering because she nurtured Love in her bosom. Or Love
is described as a captive, bound in return for his
own binding fetters.

Two from Meleager are typical: [26]

" If thou scorch so often the soul that flutters
round thee, Love, she will flee away from thee;
she too, O cruel, has wings."

" Ah, suffering Soul, now thou burnest in the
fire, and now thou revivest, and fetchest breath
again. Why weepest thou? When thou didst
nurture pitiless Love in thy bosom, knewest
thou not that he was being nurtured for thy
woe? Knewest thou not? Know now his repay-
ment, a fair foster-hire! Take it, fire and cold
snow together. Thou wouldst have it so; bear
the pain; thou sufferest the wages of thy work,
scorched with his burning honey."

Another by Crinagoras pictures Love repaid:
" Yes, weep and groan, binding together the
sinews of your hands, O Plotter. Such actions
are fitting for you. There is no one who will
relieve you. Do not cast piteous glances. For
you yourself have wrung tears from other eyes,
and have planted bitter weapons in the heart,
and have sped the arrow of desires which cannot be escaped, O Eros. And these woes of mortals caused you mirth. You have suffered what
you have caused. Noble is justice."

An epigram, by Alcaeus, of the second century B.C., has an allusion to a statue of Love in
fetters, interesting because it shows that the art
of the time was directly inspiring some of the
epigrams. Certainly the same concepts of Eros
and Psyche appear in Greek literature and art
and persist down into Roman times.

The oldest known work of art on which the
pair is represented is probably a bronze relief,
Corinthian work of the fourth century B.C. Eros
and Psyche are boy and girl, fully clothed, but
with bird wings. Eros is touching Psyche's chin
with one hand, and the two stand side by side.
The latest representation of the two of which
the date is certain is a mosaic on the ceiling of
Santa Costanza in Rome, probably early fourth

century A.D. Between these two works of art, come statues, engraved gems, Pompeian wall paintings, funeral reliefs, both pagan and Christian, and the frescoes of the catacombs. The statues are all replicas and hard to date, but the originals belonged probably to the second and first centuries B.C. The engraved gems are not earlier than Hellenistic times. The Pompeian wall paintings belong to the first century of the Christian era. The funeral reliefs range from the first to the fourth century A.D.

Collignon, whose monograph on this subject has been the starting-point of all work since, lists twenty statues of Psyche in the museums and collections of Europe. The most common types are Psyche tortured by Love, Psyche prostrated at his feet in supplication, and Psyche embracing Eros. The beautiful statue in the Capitoline Museum which shows Psyche crouching in dread and looking up, surely belongs to the second type. The most famous group of the third type is the one in the Capitoline where the young lovers embrace with unconscious and touching tenderness. Neither has wings, but their identity is indisputable and is proved by an inferior group in the Uffizi where the postures are the same, but the figures are winged. The classic reserve of the Capitoline group is felt most clearly in contrast with Rodin's modern and impressionistic treatment of the same theme. Another motif of the epigrams, Eros in fetters, appears in a group by Aphrodisias in the Berlin Museum (about the time of the birth of Christ). Again the two are wingless. Eros' hands are bound behind his back. Psyche's hands rest on Eros' shoulders.

In the engraved gems, there are five different types according to Collignon: Psyche alone, Psyche maltreated by Eros, Psyche triumphing over Eros, the union of Psyche and Eros, and a group showing varied subjects. In the first type, Psyche is a maiden, represented sometimes veiled like Nemesis, sometimes as a young girl with butterfly wings. In the second type, Psyche is fettered by Eros, or burned by the flames of his torch, or bound and wounded by his arrow. In certain gems she is represented simply as a butterfly, tormented by the wild boy Eros, who pursues butterfly with net, roasts it over a spit, nails it to a tree, or burns it with his torch. In the third type, the tables are turned, and Psyche is tormenting Eros, who appears fettered or wounded, guarded by a butterfly. In type four, many of the gems resemble the Capitoline group of sculpture. One famous gem of this class is the sardonyx cameo carved by Tryphon (Boston Museum), a little marriage scene, where one Eros with a long torch leads the tiny pair to the marriage couch which another Eros is uncovering. Eros clasps a dove to his breast. Psyche is a maiden in long robes with butterfly wings. The fifth series includes many variations of the familiar themes. For example, in one gem, Eros, acting as charioteer for Dionysus in his revels, drives two Psyches yoked to draw the god. Another shows Psyche holding a sleeping baby-Eros in her lap.

Collignon thinks that both statues and gems show a simple allegory: the struggle of the soul against its desires, sometimes victorious, sometimes vanquished, finally re-united to love; and that later the myth, transported to the funeral monuments, assumed a deeper meaning, — a hope in the future life and the happiness of the soul after death. Although Collignon may push allegorical interpretation too far, surely back of these representations of Eros and Psyche in epigrams and art did hover the vague, Platonic mysticism.

In some of the gems, several Eroses appear together. This multiplication of both Loves and

ENGRAVED GEMS

Psyches is seen in the Pompeian wall paintings
in the House of the Vettii. The decorations of
this house belong to the so-called fourth period
of Pompeian wall decoration, but show two distinct periods of composition and technique. The
paintings on our subject are in the earlier style.
They are on the walls of a large room off the
peristyle. Its decorative scheme shows the usual
threefold division of the wall. The ground of the
base is black; the main part of the wall is red,
divided into panels containing floating figures;
the upper portion shows architectural elements
against a white background. The most beautiful
part of the decoration is the frieze of Cupids and
Psyches, in a narrow strip (nine to ten inches
wide) below the panels. The Loves and Psyches
are engaged in all the occupations of the Pom-
peians of the time. Cupids make and sell gar-
lands of roses; some make olive oil; some are
goldsmiths, others fullers, others wine mer-
chants. Two distinctly Roman scenes represent
the races of the Circus and a festival of Vesta.
Below this frieze are several tiny pictures which
contain groups of Psyches gathering flowers.
While these pictures are all distinctly genre in
style, the identity of the Loves and Psyches is
never lost and the charm of a fairy story per-

meates the pictures of the little fays even at their humblest tasks.

Very different is the use of Eros and Psyche on the funeral monuments. Here the use of the myth which runs through at least four centuries is symbolic of a belief in immortality. Psyche here represents the life of the soul. Five different types appear on the pagan monuments of the first and second centuries A.D.: the soul entering into the future life; the trials of the soul purified by the divine love; the re-union of Cupid and Psyche; the association of the myth of Psyche with the story of Prometheus; the motivating use of the myth with other stories.

In the first type, there are as varied conceptions as a butterfly flying up from a skeleton and Psyche, a maiden, bearing a bust of a dead person. The central idea is the conception of the soul separated from and surviving the body. In the second type, the trials of the soul in preparation for final happiness are represented, and Psyche is tortured by Eros as in statues and gems. In the third type, the theme of the Capitoline group, the young lovers embracing, is used to typify the eternal happiness of the soul. While the execution of the figures is often crude, there is an attempt to express supreme ecstasy.

In the fourth type, the myth of Psyche is associated with that of Prometheus, the creator of man, in an allegory of birth and death. A fine sarcophagus in the Capitoline Museum illustrates this combination. In the fifth group, the Eros-Psyche story motivates the use of other myths (Diana and Endymion, Phaedra, Adonis, Mars and Rhea Silvia) and thus the thought of eternal happiness is doubly emphasized by two stories.

The Christian monuments on which Psyche figures are sarcophagi found in Christian cemeteries, and decorative paintings and mosaics in churches and catacombs. They date from the second to the fourth century A.D. The familiar pagan type of Eros and Psyche embracing appears on several sarcophagi, on one with a representation of the Good Shepherd, on another with the story of Jonah. The myth is used of course to signify the idea of resurrection and eternal happiness and its adoption suggests how faint was the boundary line between Paganism at its decline and Christianity at its birth. The same assimilation of pagan and Christian ideas is seen on a Christian sarcophagus in the Lateran where Eros and Psyche in the midst of some Bacchic genii are occupied with the work of

the vintage. All the pagan thought of Bacchus
is gone, for the scene represents " the true vine "
of the Christian God, and Psyche plucking the
grapes symbolizes the happiness of the Christian in the next world.

In the Catacombs of Domitilla near the Via
Appia among the often repeated Christian
themes of Daniel in the lions' den, Noah and his
ark, Jonah in the whale's mouth, and the Good
Shepherd, there is one small room which contains three exquisite third century frescoes of
Cupid and Psyche gathering flowers. The two
dainty young creatures with wings of bird and
butterfly are fair symbols of eternal happiness
for Christians as for pagans.

In this spirit was conceived the ceiling mosaic
of Santa Costanza, where on white ground each
in a little separate panel many small Cupids and
five tiny Psyches dance. Pysche is a young girl
in exquisite rose robe or with floating rose scarf,
always with delicate butterfly wings, and always
dancing happily, a graceful symbol of eternal
joy.

Such are the appearances of Eros and Psyche
in ancient art. Sculpture, gems, wall paintings,
funeral monuments, mosaics all use the myth in
the same vague outlines, but no trace of Apu-

THE PROMETHEUS SARCOPHAGUS
In the Capitoline Museum

leius' romance appears. Yet as the representations of Eros and Psyche vary from figures of
two small children to adolescent lovers, it may
be that in the lad-maid type of the Eros-Psyche
tale the way was prepared for attaching the
names of the God of Love and the Winged Soul
to the lovers in that old fairy tale which Apuleius re-created.

## 2. Certain Uses in Renaissance and Modern Art

THE pictorial quality of Apuleius' story of
Cupid and Psyche was recognized in the dawn
of the Italian Renaissance. Apuleius' *Meta-*
*morphoses* was one of the earliest works published, as the first edition came out in Rome in
1469 and its popularity was immediate. The
appeal of the Cupid-Psyche tale to artists has
been so great from the time of Raphael to the
present that it is impossible even to list the
varied and repeated uses of the story. An idea
of the decorative possibilities in the handling
of Apuleius' episodes may be given by a description of a few of the earliest and most
famous treatments.

So far as we know, it was Raphael who first

used Apuleius' narrative in art. This was in the
Villa Farnesina in Rome. Vasari tells the romantic conditions under which the artist designed these great frescoes. " We find it related
that his intimate friend Agostino Chigi had
commissioned him to paint the first floor of his
palace, but Raphael was at that time so much
occupied with the love which he bore to the
lady of his choice, that he could not give sufficient attention to the work. Agostino, therefore, falling at length into despair of seeing it
finished, made so many efforts by means of
friends and by his own care, that after much
difficulty he at length prevailed on the lady to
take up her abode in his house, where she was
accordingly installed in apartments near those
which Raphael was painting; in this manner
the work was ultimately brought to a conclusion." [27] Raphael, as Apuleius himself would
say, " Sponte in Amoris incidit amorem, tunc
magis magisque cupidine flagrans Cupidinis,"
and out of his own passion re-created the passion of Cupid and Psyche with such superb
inspiration that artist after artist followed his
work.

The portico of the Farnesina furnished to
Raphael three different surfaces for decoration:

the great, rectangular ceiling; on the sides, the spandrels of the arches above the pilasters; and in the intervals between the pilasters the arches which unite them. On the arches are many Amorini who bear the weapons and symbols of the Olympian gods. The story of Psyche herself is told in twelve compositions, ten in the triangular spandrels, two on the ceiling. The selection of episodes is so influential in future treatment that it is well to list the subjects here.

1. Venus angrily pointing out Psyche, her earthly rival, to Cupid.

2. Cupid imploring the Graces to protect his love, Psyche. (Not in Apuleius.)

3. Venus imploring aid from Juno and Ceres for her vengeance upon Psyche.

4. Venus, charioted by doves, ascending to Olympus.

5. Venus begging Jupiter's aid.

6. Mercury descending from heaven to proclaim that no one is to shelter Psyche, the fugitive slave of Venus.

7. Psyche, borne aloft by Cupids, carrying vase from Proserpina to Venus.

8. Psyche, kneeling before Venus, presenting Proserpina's gift.

9. Cupid telling Jupiter the story of his love.

10. Mercury escorting Psyche to Olympus.

On the ceiling are two great rectangular scenes, the Council of the Gods in Heaven, the Marriage of Cupid and Psyche.

A visit to the Villa Farnesina today brings disappointment because in the first place Raphael's designs were executed by his pupils, Penni and Giulio Romano, and, secondly, in the eighteenth century the frescoes were restored by Carlo Maratti whose work, while preserving the great originals defaced their coloring. On a dark day, when the crude blue of the background and the evident re-painting are less conspicuous, the magnificence and joy of Raphael's treatment of the story still captivate the imagination.

Two other great decorative schemes tower above all other uses of the story in art: Pierino del Vaga's in the Castle of Sant' Angelo; Giulio Romano's in the Palazzo del Tè in Mantua. Pierino del Vaga's designs for a hall in the Castle of Sant' Angelo are arranged in a frieze, in separate panels, divided by arabesque designs and connected by festoons held by Cupids. The frieze is high on the wall below an ornate ceiling. Del Vaga in his designs was indebted both to his master, Raphael, and to a Flemish painter, Michiel van Coxie, who made thirty-two drawings illustrating the story of Cupid and Psyche. There are nine panels.

1. In front of the robbers' cave, the old hag begins to the stolen bride, Charite, the story of Cupid and Psyche while Lucius, the ass, looks on.

2. Contains three scenes: Psyche worshipped by the people; Venus pointing out Psyche to Cupid; Psyche's father imploring aid from Apollo.

3. According to the oracle, Psyche is conducted to the mountain with funereal pomp.

4. Shows first Psyche banqueting in the Palace of Love and then couched with Love.

5. Has three scenes: Psyche examining the weapons of Love; Psyche discovering Love asleep by the aid of her lamp; Psyche attempting to cling to Love as he flies out of the window.

6. Venus upbraiding Cupid; Venus talking to Ceres and Juno.

7. Psyche tormented before Venus by Sollicitudo and Tristities. Psyche ordered to sort the grains.

8. Has several scenes: Venus giving Psyche the jar; the talking tower advising Psyche; Psyche kneeling before Proserpina; Cupid awaking Psyche from her fateful sleep.

9. The wedding banquet.

The mere listing of the subjects used by del Vaga shows the contrast between his conception and that of Raphael. Raphael, the great artist, selected those moments in the story which appealed most to the imagination and conveyed most brilliantly the Olympian grandeur of the setting. The Märchen element is virtually suppressed. The homely, the grotesque, and the painful are noticeably absent. The interest of the artist centers in the gods of Olympus and their relation to Cupid's love story, not in the suffering of a mortal girl. The story is told for the most part by scenes in which groups of only two or three persons appear. Simplicity of design and joy of mood unite to produce the room's beauty.

Del Vaga in contrast is a painstaking, faithful imitator of Apuleius, using a narrative style which demands many details. Psyche is here the center of the story. Incongruously enough, as in van Coxie, the lover Cupid is a mere child. The grotesque attempt of Psyche to cling to Cupid's ankle as he flies out of the window is also taken over from van Coxie. Magic has its place, for the talking tower is visualized. Del Vaga in short is an illustrator of Apuleius and

[ 176 ]

an imitator of Raphael and of van Coxie, not a great creative artist.

Giulio Romano's work in the Palazzo del Tè is far more sensuous than that of Raphael or of del Vaga and emphasizes the amorous element in the story. The room, which is very large, has a ceiling covered with oil paintings rich and dark in coloring, separated by heavy, gilded mouldings, while the side walls are decorated with larger and brighter pictures in fresco. In the center of the ceiling is Olympus, depth on depth of golden light, with Jupiter witness of the nuptials of Cupid and Psyche, which are symbolized in four paintings, half octagons, about the central panel. The other designs of the ceiling are arranged in concentric circles of different shaped panels. Next come octagonal pictures in which some of the scenes are the King consulting the Oracle, the people worshipping Psyche, Cupid pointing out Psyche to Venus, Psyche borne through the air by Zephyr, Psyche entertaining her sisters, Psyche discovering Cupid. Around these octagons is a set of small pointed lunettes containing Amorini, and outside of these, twelve semicircular pictures of Psyche's tasks. On the side walls are two large frescoes, one the preparations for the

[ 177 ]

wedding feast, the other the feast itself. Such a list of subjects gives no conception of the magnificence of the room, the voluptuous richness of detail, the glamour and the delicacy of some of the individual scenes, most of all the one where Psyche raises her light and discovers the sleeping God.

For faithful illustration of Apuleius' narrative, the thirty-two designs of Michiel van Coxie, a sixteenth century Flemish painter, are the most notable. These may be seen in the engravings of Agostino Veneziano in the Bibliothéque Nationale, Départment des Estampes, Paris.[28] Any lover of the story will find it worth while to get permission to see these delightful line drawings, so full of Apuleius' charm and spirit. It is noteworthy that throughout these thirty-two designs Cupid is a child. Yet the love motif in the story is emphasized. The fairy-tale element is as conspicuous as the Olympian atmosphere. Van Coxie furnished designs not only for del Vaga's frescoes in Rome, but for works of far different technique and habitat, for example, the stained glass windows of the Gallerie de Psychè, in the Château de Chantilly, and the Brussels tapestries in the Vassar College Library.

PSYCHE DISCOVERS CUPID

Engraved by Agostino Veneziano from the design of Michiel van Coxie

A study of these uses of the Cupid and Psyche story is a preparation for recognition and enjoyment of countless other uses of the story in Renaissance and modern times. In palaces, in museums of Europe and America, even in a great New York hotel the story is used repeatedly in mural decoration, in oil paintings, on cassone panels. In Italy alone, many other artists have used these motifs: Giovanni Francesco, Francesco Menzochi, Parmi Gianina, Francesco Salviati, Taddeo Zucchero, Titian, Correggio, Caravaggio, and a host of others. In France, Natoire, Gerard, David, Prud'hon, Baudry are among the most noted artists who have used the tale. Distinguished painters of other countries who have adopted these subjects are Rubens, Velasquez and Van Dyck. Familiarity with the story is rewarded by repeated meetings with illustrations of it.

The story was not only painted but woven in textiles. In the history of tapestry making, the Cupid and Psyche story is found to be the subject of some of the most famous series. There are early Gobelin tapestries with Cupid-Psyche designs influenced by both Raphael and Giulio Romano. Later, when Boucher came to the Gobelins from the Beauvais Tapestry Works, he designed another Cupid and Psyche series for the Gobelins. Boucher had already designed a Cupid and Psyche set for the Beauvais Works (1741–70) which included five scenes: Psyche arriving at Cupid's Palace, Psyche abandoned by Cupid, Psyche's Toilet, Psyche at the Basket-Maker's, Psyche displaying her treasures to her sisters. Boucher followed La Fontaine's rendering of the story, but contemporized Psyche with the Court of Louis XV and the taste of the Marquise de Pompadour.

Belgium as well as France produced Cupid and Psyche tapestries. The Metropolitan Museum in New York has a famous set woven at Brussels in the second half of the sixteenth century. The scenes are:

1. The bath of Psyche.

2. The banquet of Psyche, with a second scene above: Cupid and Psyche on the couch.

3. The largest, containing three scenes: the jealous sisters taunting Psyche; Psyche discovering Cupid; Cupid flying out of the window with Psyche clinging to his ankle.

4. The visit of the sisters to Psyche, first flying through the air, then seeing her treasures.

5. Psyche's visit to the lower world, first

giving a cake to Cerberus, secondly presenting the jar to Proserpina.

There is another large Brussels tapestry of the early eighteenth century in the New York Public Library which depicts the marriage feast of Cupid and Psyche, using part of Raphael's great design. The Vassar College Library has another set of five, made in Belgium in the first half of the seventeenth century. They follow the designs of van Coxie and are rarely beautiful in execution and colors.

In modern sculpture, the tendency has been away from Apuleius to the ancient conception of Love and the Soul. And the theme used is the embrace of the young lovers. Canova's group shows daintiness of handling and tenderness of feeling with something of the classic restraint but too much prettiness; Rodin's group is impressionistic in handling and impassioned in spirit, another great work.

## AVE ATQUE VALE

A FAREWELL to Apuleius should salute him not as a dead, but as a living person. This brief review of his work and influence shows that he has flourished through many generations. An inspection of the omens for the future forecasts a revival of interest in his work.

The activity of archaeological research in Africa on the part of both French and Italians must naturally be accompanied by renewed study of Roman writers born on African soil who contribute something to knowledge of the country. The economic history of Rome is now being written, and for this, new studies of the economic life of the province of Africa are indispensable. To these Apuleius is bound to contribute much, just as he has already proved a priceless source for knowledge of Roman jurisprudence. For the student of ancient magic, religion, and philosophy he paints a picture without parallel for the second century of the Roman Empire. For the student of the literary history of Rome he affords illustration of the development of juridical and sophistic oratory, and for students and readers of novels and short stories in all languages his *Metamorphoses* is a unique work in the development of romance.

The history of the various periods of his influence is significant. His doctrine of demonology and incubation, so revered in the Middle Ages, is no longer popular, although it has had a strange revival in a cult of the nineteenth century. His Platonic writings are mere curiosities now, since the idealists of today do not need Latin versions of Plato's works. His voluminous scientific works, bound to be of ephemeral interest with the progress of knowledge, are lost. But his romance since the time when it was re-discovered and acclaimed by the Renaissance has found readers and imitators in every epoch. With the taste of different ages, various elements have attained greater popularity: now the literature of the ass, now the Milesian tales, now the fairy Märchen. But through the centuries, that pearl of great price, the tale of Cupid and Psyche, has been given one new setting after another in literature and art; and still shines the fairest jewel in the crown of this prince of story-tellers.

# NOTES

1.  Two passages in Apuleius (*Met.*, vii. 13 *virginem asino triumphantem* and *Met.*, ix. 14 *praesumptione dei, quem praedicaret unicum*) have been interpreted as satirical references to Christianity. This exegesis does not seem justified.

2.  Alexander Graham, *Roman Africa*, p. 189.

2a. Recently the Americans have joined with the French. Cf. Kelsey, " A Preliminary Report on the Excavations at Carthage," Suppl. to *A. J. A.* 1926.

3.  *Apuleius*, in *The Loeb Classical Library*, p. xxiii.

4.  See table of Greek Novels in S. L. Wolff, *Greek Romances in Elizabethan Prose Fiction*, New York, 1912, pp. 8–10.

5.  J. W. Mackail's poem, " Cupid and Psyche."

6.  In this section I am indebted, largely, to Schanz, *Geschichte der röm. Litteratur* and to L. C. Purser.

7.  *De Civ. Dei*, VIII. 12.

8.  *Inst.*, V. 3.

9.  *Inst.*, II. 15.

10. XII. 12.

11. Hier. on Psalm LXXXI, Apoll. Sid., *Ep.*, II. 10.5; IV. 3. 1.

12. *Ep.*, 102. 32; 138. 18–19; *De Civ. Dei*, VIII. 12–22, XVIII. 18.

13. *De Civ. Dei*, XV. 23, transl. by M. Dods.

14. *Dial.*, I. 4.

15. Migne, XCIV, Bede, V. p. 843.

16. " Apulée magicien," in *Rev. des deux mondes*, LXXXV. 607–8 (1888).

17. *Anth. Pal.*, II. 303.

18. *Bull. de corr. hell.*, I. p. 131.

19. Manitius, II. pp. 635–6.

20. Manitius, II. p. 489.
21. *Historia regum Britanniae*, Book VI, Chapters 17–18.
22. *Renaissance in Italy*, II. p. 71.
23. *Cabala*, p. 563. 12.
24. V. 22.
25. Book III, canto 6.
26. J. W. Mackail's translations are used: *Select Epigrams from the Greek Anthology*, London and New York, 1911.
27. *Lives of Seventy of the Most Eminent Painters, Sculptors and Architects*, Giorgio Vasari, edited by E. H. and E. W. Blashfield and A. A. Hopkins, 4 vols., New York, 1923, III. p. 201.
28. There is another set in the New York Public Library.

All translations, unless otherwise specified, are those of E. H. H. The editors of " Art and Archaeology " and of " Poet Lore " have kindly allowed me to use portions of my essays published in those periodicals.

# BIBLIOGRAPHY

I.  Editions and Translations into English.

ADLINGTON, W., (1566) revised by GASELEE, S., *Apuleius: The Golden Ass,* Translation with Latin text, in *The Loeb Classical Library.* New York, 1915.

BUTLER, H. E., *The Apologia and Florida,* 1909, *The Metamorphoses.* 2 vols. 1910, (translation), Oxford.

——, and OWEN, A. S., (editors), *Apologia.* Oxford, 1914.

HELM, R., (editor), *Apulei opera quae supersunt.* Leipsic, 1912, 1913, 1921.

OUDENDORP, F. VAN, and HILDEBRAND, G. F., (editors), *L. Apulei opera omnia.* Leipsic, 1842.

PURSER, L. C., (editor), *The Story of Cupid and Psyche as related by Apuleius.* London, 1910.

STUTTAFORD, CHARLES, *Apuleius: The Story of Cupid and Psyche,* (translation). London, 1903.


II.  Articles and Books on Apuleius.

Abt, A., *Die Apologie des Apuleius von Madaura und die antike Zauberei.* Giessen, 1907.

COCCHIA, ENRICO, *Romanzo e realtà nella vita — e nell' attività letteraria di Lucio Apuleio.* Catania, 1915.

DE JONG, K. H. E., *De Apuleio isiacorum mysteriorum teste* (Dissertation). Leyden, 1900.

KRÜGER, G., *Kritische Ausgabe.* Berlin, 1865.

LANG, ANDREW, *Custom and Myth.* New York, 1885.

MONCEAUX, PAUL, *Apulée. Roman et magie.* Paris, 1888.

NORDEN, FRITZ, *Apulejus von Madaura und das römische Privatrecht.* Leipsic, 1912.

PERRY, BEN EDWIN, *The Metamorphoses ascribed to Lucius of Patrae.* (Princeton University Dissertation) Lancaster, Pa., 1920.

# BIBLIOGRAPHY

ROHDE, E., *Der griechische Roman und seine Vorläufer.* Leipsic, 1900.

——, *Kleine Schriften.* Leipsic, 1901.

SCHANZ, M., *Geschichte der römischen Litteratur,* VIII. 3, pp. 103–144. Munich, 1905.

TEUFFEL, W. S., and SCHWABE, L., *History of Roman Literature,* translation by G. C. W. Warr. 2 vols. London, 1900.

THORNDIKE, LYNN, *A History of Magic and Experimental Science during the First Thirteen Centuries of our Era.* 2 vols. New York, 1923.

——, "Apuleius," in *Encyclopaedia Britannica,* Vol. II, pp. 234–5. 1910.

ZINZOW, ADOLF, *Psyche und Eros.* Halle A. S., 1881.


III. Roman Africa.

BOISSIER, G., *Roman Africa,* translation by A. Ward. New York, 1899.

BOUCHIER, E. S., *Life and Letters in Roman Africa.* Oxford, 1913.

GRAHAM, ALEXANDER, *Roman Africa.* London, 1902.

GRANT, CYRIL FLETCHER, and GRANT, L., *'Twixt Sand and Sea, Sketches and Studies in North Africa.* London, 1911.

GSELL, STÉPHANE, *Histoire ancienne de l'Afrique du Nord.* 4 vols. Paris, 1913–1920.


IV. Apuleius in the Middle Ages.

HUET, G., "Le roman d'Apulée était-il connu au moyen âge?" in *Le moyen âge,* 2e Série. XIII. 23–28 (1909).

KAWCZYNSKI, M., "Ist Apuleius im Mittelalter bekannt gewesen?" in *Bausteine zur romanischen Philologie,* XLVII. 193–210 (1905).

LACROIX, PAUL, *Science and Literature in the Middle Ages and at the Period of the Rennaissance,* pp. 240–9. London, 1878.

MANITIUS, M., *Geschichte der lateinischen Litteratur des Mittelalters.* 2 vols. Munich, 1911, 1923.

[ 188 ]

——, "*Philologisches aus alten Bibliothekskatalogen*," in *Rheinisches Museum*, XLVII. Sup., 1–152 (1892).

MONCEAUX, PAUL, "Apulée magicien," in *Révue des deux mondes*, LXXXV. 571–608 (1888).

NITZE, W. A., and DARGAN, E. P., *A History of French Literature*, Part I. New York, 1922.

SANDYS, J. E., *A History of Classical Scholarship*. 3 vols. Cambridge, England, 1903–1908.

WEYMAN, CARL, "Studien zu Apuleius und seinen Nachahmern," in *Sitzungsb. d. Akad. d. Wiss. zu München*, II. 321–392 (1893).


V. Apuleius in the Renaissance and Modern Times.

BLÜMNER, H., "Das Märchen von Amor und Psyche in der deutschen Dichtkunst," in *Neue Jahrbücher für das klassische Altertum*, XI. 648–673 (1903).

HAIGHT, E. H., "Introducing Apuleius," "On Certain Uses of Apuleius' Story of Cupid and Psyche in English Literature," in *Poet Lore*, XXVI, no. 6. 694–706, 744–762 (1915).

HELM, R., "Das 'Märchen' von Amor und Psyche," in *Neue Jahrbücher für das klassische Altertum*, XXXIII. 170–209 (1914).

HOFFMANN, ADOLF, *Das Psyche-Märchen des Apuleius in der englischen Litteratur*. (Thesis) Strassburg, 1908.

PATER, WALTER, *Marius the Epicurean*. New York, 1907.

SPAMPANATO, VINCENZO, *Giordano Bruno e la letteratura dell' asino*. Portici, Della Torre, 1904.

STUMFALL, BALTHASAR, *Das Märchen von Amor und Psyche in seinem Fortleben in der französischen italienischen und spanischen Literatur bis zum 18 Jahrhundert*. Münchener Beitrag, xxxix, 1907.


VI. The Story of Cupid and Psyche in Art.

COLLIGNON, M., *Essai sur les monuments grecs et romains relatifs au mythe de Psyché*. Paris, 1877.

DAREMBERG, C. V., ET SAGLIO, E., *Dictionnaire des antiquités grecques et romaines*. 5 vols. Paris, 1877–1919.

# BIBLIOGRAPHY

DE MARIA, UGO, *La favola di Amore e Psiche nella letter-atura e nell' arte italiana.* Bologna, 1899.

FURTWÄNGLER, A., *Die antiken Gemmen.* Leipsic, 1900.

HAIGHT, E. H., " The Myth of Cupid and Psyche in Ancient Art," in *Art and Archaeology*, III. 43–52, 87–97 (1916) ; " The Myth of Cupid and Psyche in Renaissance Art," " The Vassar College Psyche Tapestries," in *Art and Archaeology*, XV. 107–116 (1923).

HUNTER, G. L., " Beauvais-Boucher Tapestries," in *Arts and Decoration*, X. 244–8, 319–21 ; XI. 28–9 (1919).

——, *Tapestries, Their Origin, History and Renaissance.* New York, 1913.

REINACH, S., *Répertoire de la statuaire grecque et romaine.* 4 vols. Paris, 1897.

ROSCHER, W. H., *Ausführliches Lexikon der griechischen und römischen Mythologie*, Vol. III. 2. Leipsic, 1902–9.

Our Debt to Greece and Rome

AUTHORS AND TITLES

# AUTHORS AND TITLES

Homer. *John A. Scott.*

Sappho. *David M. Robinson.*

Euripides. *F. L. Lucas.*

Aristophanes. *Louis E. Lord.*

Demosthenes. *Charles D. Adams.*

The Poetics of Aristotle. *Lane Cooper.*

Greek Rhetoric and Literary Criticism. *W. Rhys Roberts.*

Lucian. *Francis G. Allinson.*

Cicero and His Influence. *John C. Rolfe.*

Catullus. *Karl P. Harrington.*

Lucretius and His Influence. *George Depue Hadzsits.*

Ovid. *Edward Kennard Rand.*

Horace. *Grant Showerman.*

Virgil. *John William Mackail.*

Seneca The Philosopher. *Richard Mott Gummere.*

Apuleius. *Elizabeth Hazelton Haight.*

Martial. *Paul Nixon.*

Platonism. *Alfred Edward Taylor.*

Aristotelianism. *John L. Stocks.*

Stoicism. *Robert Mark Wenley.*

Language and Philology. *Roland G. Kent.*

# AUTHORS AND TITLES